THE LIVES OF DILLON RIPLEY

THE LIVES OF
DILLON
RIPLEY

NATURAL SCIENTIST, WARTIME SPY,
AND PIONEERING LEADER OF THE
SMITHSONIAN INSTITUTION

Roger D. Stone

ForeEdge

ForeEdge

An imprint of University Press of New England

www.upne.com

© 2017 Sustainable Development Institute

All rights reserved

Manufactured in the United States of America

Designed by April Leidig

Typeset in Ehrhardt by Copperline Book Services

For permission to reproduce any of the material in this book,
contact Permissions, University Press of New England,
One Court Street, Suite 250, Lebanon NH 03766;
or visit www.upne.com

Hardcover ISBN: 978-1-61168-656-2

Ebook ISBN: 978-1-5126-0061-2

Library of Congress Cataloging-in-Publication Data
available on request

5 4 3 2 1

Contents

Foreword

TOM LOVEJOY

When I entered the Peabody Museum on the afternoon of my first day as a Yale undergraduate, I was thrilled. I loved natural history and knew the Peabody, but I had little inkling of what it might lead to. That afternoon I met my freshman adviser, Philip Humphrey, assistant curator of birds, who in 1965 would set me on my course in the Amazon. Within a week I met the director, S. Dillon Ripley, and was volunteering in the Bird Division.

My initial reaction to the six-foot-four-inch gentleman was one of awe, but he was also welcoming. His balding pate led me to think he was considerably older than he was, but that impression was dispelled the following week when I saw him take the Peabody stairs two at a time.

This was an exciting time at the Peabody. The bird collections were being moved out of the Peabody's tower into the top floor of the brand-new Bingham wing. Hardly a month later, as a very green freshman, I was able to attend the official opening of the Bingham Oceanographic and Ornithological Laboratory (O&O) presided over by the elegant director, with an address by President Griswold and another by the wizardlike G. Evelyn Hutchinson on the value of museums and the puzzle of why there might be so many green pigeons.

As a sophomore I took Ripley and Humphrey's ornithology course, soaking up every morsel of knowledge imparted, whether in class or in the field. I became one of a small cadre of Peabody undergraduates encouraged by welcoming curators and always led by the sophisticated director. Ripley was simultaneously a gentleman of the world and an inveterate field naturalist who would vanish to exotic parts of the world like New Guinea or India.

For many of us, he was an exemplar of someone who could be at home in, and explore, nature but also be wise to the human "ways of the world"—and always with a sense of fun and whimsy, as when he and his close friend and scientific colleague, Sálim Ali, availed themselves of an opportunity to taste elephant milk (their report: it tasted chalky) or when in my senior year he arranged for a belly dancer to perform at the black tie dinner in the Peabody Great Hall celebrating the *King Tut's Treasures* exhibition.

With the Peabody's and Ripley's encouragement I did what was then unheard of and took a year off (between junior and senior years) to go on a Peabody expedition to Nubia when the Aswan Dam was under construction. By the time I returned my fate was sealed: I was to be a field biologist. But I also soon heard a rumor that Ripley would be leaving Yale to become the next secretary of the Smithsonian Institution. How exciting it was to personally know the new secretary—but that was another world.

Ripley had an incredible memory for just about everything. For example, I learned from him that there is a tattoo museum in Japan. Mary Ripley, his amazing wife, who shared his passion for the natural world, once said that being married to him was like being married to an encyclopedia. That memory also applied to people: he did not forget friends, nor did he forget their interests and talents.

That interest in people was to bring our paths together again when I came to the World Wildlife Fund in 1973. Ripley believed that every biologist with a conscience should spend time on conservation—that conservation was a hallmark of civilization. David Challinor, who had been recruited by Ripley to be assistant secretary of science at the Smithsonian, tipped me off as to a job possibility that led to fourteen years at WWF.

That same interest in people, their interests and abilities also made him a superb Smithsonian secretary. Regardless of the energies he put into cultivating Congress, or drawing President Johnson to a White House window to suggest that the Smithsonian acquire the historic building that became the Renwick Gallery (of the Smithsonian Museum of American Art), or hobnobbing and fundraising, he never forgot for an instant what the Smithsonian was really about: collections and scholars. Many a curator or researcher would get a call directly from the secretary eager to learn about the latest scholarship or exhibition.

With all his respect for scholarship, Ripley felt that visiting museums should be fun rather than intimidating. Far from being dismayed that the Smithsonian was characterized as the "nation's attic," his view was that it was where one went to play on a rainy day. Of historical musical instruments: "Take the instruments from their cases and let them sing." The museums embraced the Million Man March on the Mall, and the Folk Life Festival brought the Mall to life, perhaps most memorably with the Festival of India.

There is no question that Ripley's secretaryship was the greatest in the twentieth century and equaled only by Joseph Henry's in the entire sweep of Smithsonian history. He was in so many ways the perfect person for his era; certainly he made the most of it.

For quite a while the prospect of writing a biography was so daunting that it seemed nobody would be up to or willing to take it on. It is more than fortunate that Roger Stone, as dedicated an environmentalist as Dillon Ripley, but also a highly skilled writer who grasped the values of the complex man, has given us a portrait worthy of the subject.

Introduction

For twenty years, from 1964 to 1984, the ornithologist Sidney Dillon Ripley held the world's top cultural job as head of the sprawling Smithsonian Institution in Washington, DC. In itself, this position was a major challenge and opportunity. For the energetic Ripley, his work as the Smithsonian's secretary (CEO) was chief among myriad other achievements as a scientist, nature conservationist, teacher, humanist, museum activist, spy, international affairs practitioner, gifted fundraiser, and waterfowl breeder.

Our subject set standards and goals for cultural and scientific institutions that current leaders and observers, half a century later, continue to admire. He exercised unilateral control over a cultural complex that during his reign became the world's largest and most visited of its kind. He left behind a vivid and well-illustrated but insufficiently known trove of information about his frequent adventures in far-off places and rich life at homes in the US Northeast. No one had yet tried to set forth, in a single volume, the full course of this man's charmed life and multiple skills. To this author, who shares Ripley's values, it seemed a worthy challenge.

Ripley was a diligent scientist in the field and in the lab. He was a pioneer in the emerging field of ecology, working globally at top levels to raise cries of alarm about disturbing losses in our planet's variety and number of plants and animals. He made a strong case for why scientists needed to be outspoken conservationists. Unlike many scientists, he was a gifted writer of books and articles for the general public as well as for academic peers. An innovative museum official, a standard-bearer, Ripley urged managers and curators at the Smithsonian and elsewhere in the museum world, often contentedly passive custodians of musty collections, to become outward-looking education proponents in art- and science-museum communities. The Smithsonian flourished and grew at a record pace during the years he was in charge.

A registered Republican, he was a liberal patrician in the style of some Roosevelts, Rockefellers, and Harrimans. He often moved in elegant circles within which he knew everybody. He loved clubs, parties, and ceremonies. He displayed respect for a diverse array of people, from museum guards and Papuan chieftains to Indian potentates and obscure graduate students, always wanting to know what they were doing and why. He had endless curiosity and a wicked sense of humor. There was a whiff of Cecil B. DeMille about him. Such was the velvet softness of his touch that he could have been a distinguished and distinctive ambassador or college president, or a gifted actor. Almost six feet four, skinny, he had a football-shaped head that reminded some people of a pelican's and others of Noel Coward's. He was, eulogized the biologist Tom Lovejoy, a "splendidly delicious" man.

Some regarded him as intimidating, imperious, self-absorbed, an empire builder. He could make life difficult for those outside his inner circle. He could turn icy. But most people who helped him, and there were many, thought it a grand privilege to work for this man. Those he knew who survive still respectfully refer to "Mr. Ripley"—he disliked using his "Dr."—or the "Sun King." Not even now would many of them call him "Dillon." From peers and bosses he earned mostly top marks for his multiple high-wire victories, his gracious charm, and his ability to deflect criticism. He was "the most sophisticated guy I ever knew," said Fisher Howe, a widely acquainted wartime intelligence colleague.[1]

Ripley as a child was happily spoiled by a much older brother, two older sisters, and an adventuresome mother. In the US Northeast he explored the nooks and crannies of Kilvarock, the sixty-one-room, nine-bedroom family castle in Litchfield, the woodsy little town in northern Connecticut, near the Berkshire Mountains, where family members still live and spend summers. He also had a keen appetite for travels to distant lands, first-class aboard the luxurious ocean liners of the 1920s and 1930s, and in residence at Claridge's in London or maharajas' palaces in India or a tented camp near the Pyramids. He loved luxury and pageantry and high culture, this coddled man. He also tolerated severe hardship. During lengthy ornithological expeditions deep into the backlands of Asia and the South Pacific, he remained cheerful even when felled by heavy bouts of malaria or dysentery, or when battling leeches, cold weather at high altitudes, heat, or torrential downpours. "Fun" was a word he frequently used, though to all but the most intrepid voyagers some of his travels were an acquired taste.

In 1964, at age forty-nine, he entered his golden Smithsonian era, the ten-year span during which he scored several of his most dramatic achievements. Many of Ripley's greatest successes had their origin in Lyndon B. Johnson's Great Society, a broad redefinition of American values extending far beyond the provision of new health benefits. Ripley was directly or mostly responsible for each of the Smithsonian projects highlighted in these pages. Each carries with it a lively story, with Ripley often starting from scratch and usually somehow winning, often against long odds, as he sought to establish greater visibility and prestige for the Smithsonian. This book raises central questions about why and how the charismatic Mr. Ripley became a distinguished leader in so many fields, his enjoyment of life's precious moments along the way, and the broader significance of his accomplishments. After summarizing the criticism that inevitably built up in opposition to Ripley's aggressive activism, the book in its closing sections sets forth a balance sheet.

The Ripley record is well documented in his own extensive writings, in a comprehensive set of oral history interviews that were audiotaped in increments from 1977 to 1993, and in copious boxes of materials stored at the Smithsonian Institution Archives near the Mall. After he left the Smithsonian in 1984, he started to assemble his written memoirs, but he had completed only fragments of this work before illness overcame him. He died in 2001 at age eighty-seven.

During midcentury periods when family finances wobbled, Ripley turned to the typewriter, publishing well-written trade books and magazine articles about his globe-trotting adventures. The author of four popular books, several hundred scientific publications, and countless articles and memoranda and speeches, Ripley could claim a successful life simply on the basis of his prolific writings. *Trail of the Money Bird* covers his 1936–37 transpacific sailboat ride and subsequent treks into remote corners of New Guinea. In *Search for the Spiny Babbler*, we join him on two tiring post–World War II bird-collecting expeditions to Nepal. *A Paddling of Ducks* covers a lifetime of passionate interest in his Litchfield duck-breeding ponds and close linkage with other prominent people who raised waterfowl elsewhere. In *The Sacred Grove: Essays on Museums* he suggests ways for museums to become more energetic and less like "cozy cemeteries of the past."[2]

From time to time, researchers have culled the Ripley archive to showcase parts of the Ripley saga. An example is the environmental historian Michael Lewis's *Inventing Global Ecology*, originally a doctoral dissertation that grew into a scholarly book on international scientific relations in India during the post–World War II period of mounting anticolonialism on the subcontinent. William Walker's book *A Living Exhibition* champions many of Ripley's proactive ideas about museums' role as educators. My book, gathering information from these and many other sources across a broad spectrum, uses exemplary case studies to suggest how this soft-voiced but steely man did so much so well and with such zest. It covers the highlights, sketching in the details of how the magical Mr. Ripley flicked on lights as he progressed across life's stage, broadening and deepening his outlook as he skipped along.

There is a personal note to add, for my attraction to the subject results in part from some similarities between the course of Ripley's life experience and my own. I, too, knew a Yale where scientists as well as birds were seated below the salt. In a succession of incarnations—as a pilot in the conservative navy of the 1950s, later as a correspondent and news bureau chief for Henry Luce's *Time* magazine, and as a bank and nonprofit executive under David Rockefeller's guidance—I had been exposed to conventional rankings of importance. Politics, economics, and security issues seemed always to trump environmental considerations. At the World Wildlife Fund I later saw the world through Ripley's prism, and starting in the 1980s I accordingly sharpened the focus of my writing and thought, concentrating on species-rich tropical forest and coastal issues. Epiphany is too grand a word to describe my trajectory, but reading and learning about Ripley surely made me keen to write about his sense of what matters and to march a bit in his footsteps.

In sum, this book invites the reader to assess the legacy this man built. Was Sidney Dillon Ripley truly a self-absorbed empire builder, as some would describe him? Or was he in the best sense a public servant, expending all that energy, skill, and chutzpah in order to score broader achievements for the benefit of the widest possible range of constituencies? Was his ambition simply a question of sensing needs and developing ways to fulfill them? What made him want so eagerly to do what he did?

What made him clamber up Yale's Science Hill, where elite classmates never went, or scramble for his Harvard doctorate in zoology? What made him fearlessly trudge out to the world's least accessible edges or exhaust himself to help rescue an ailing planet when he could have enjoyed a comfortable country-squire life at his Connecticut duck sanctuary? Did he want to be famous and achieve personal glory, or were those bouquets simply thrust upon him as a byproduct of what he did? Was he lucky, brilliant, or both? When and how did noblesse oblige become a factor? How did he manage to keep detractors at bay? These are among the central questions this book poses about this endlessly delightful, enigmatic man.

CHAPTER ONE

Growing Up Golden

One of his great regrets, Ripley said, was that he never knew any of his grandparents. Born on September 20, 1913, he was the great-grandson of Sidney Dillon, the founding chair of the Union Pacific Railroad, who in 1869 drove in the ceremonial golden spike that linked the nation by rail. On that side of the family, both of Ripley's paternal grandparents had died before World War I. By then both grandparents on his mother's side had perished as well. That left one Dillon family member, Cora Dillon Wyckoff, the goodhearted, much younger sister of Ripley's grandmother Julia Dillon, as the only surviving relative from that generation.

Those who pampered Dillon Ripley during the early years of his life included not only the opulent Wyckoffs but his two much older sisters, Julie Rose Ripley and Constance Dillon Ripley, an older brother, Louis Rose Ripley, and his indefatigable mother, Constance Baillie Rose Ripley. She was a stalwart native of Kingston, Ontario, of Scottish descent, who had come to New York to study nursing at the Columbia Presbyterian Hospital and had met her husband-to-be. His father, said Dillon Ripley, had been left a substantial trust fund and income and had no incentive to follow his older brother from boarding school (Hotchkiss in northwestern Connecticut) to

Yale.[1] Instead, he dabbled in business ventures and pursued his passion for golf.

The vivacious Auntie Cora, as Ripley called her, lived with her husband, a lapsed medical doctor named Peter Wyckoff, in an apartment on New York's newly stylish Park Avenue. It had been lavishly furnished by the fashionable actress and decorator Elsie de Wolfe, famous for having had prominent clients, including the Duke and Duchess of Windsor and Henry Clay Frick. Cora Wyckoff was a warm and friendly relative, said Ripley. Throughout his life, he told the oral historian Pamela Henson, he carried vivid memories of his occasional brushes with the grand luxe standards that the Wyckoffs maintained in New York and in Long Island's sumptuous Southampton.

An afternoon at the seashore in their manner was hardly a lighthearted frolic in sun-dappled froth. The Wyckoffs' version suggested something about the pomp-and-circumstance formality of their daily lives. Invited by Auntie Cora to visit her "cottage" in Southampton, the Ripley brothers were taken to a beach picnic aboard a Renault town car, separated from the open front seat by a glass partition, and driven to the edge of the village by a chauffeur wearing solid leather puttees and a mulberry-colored uniform. "There were no caterpillars in the sandwiches, no sand, and after a while we began silently to cry, because it was not really a picnic at all," he recalled complaining to the butler.[2] It was more formal than even he, who relished luxury, could enjoy. But he loved his Auntie Cora.

A few years later, asked by the Wyckoffs for dinner in New York at the age of thirteen, Ripley and his older brother put on stiff shirts and dinner jackets and were served by a butler and footman. After the meal, as Ripley told the story, Uncle Peter repaired with the young Ripleys to a smoking room, where a butler lit up for Uncle Peter a huge, torpedo-shaped cigar. He took several huge drafts, sighed, and, cigar firmly clenched in his teeth, sank into a form of torpor as the smoldering stogie started emitting smoke signals from inside his shirt. It displayed an enlarging brown spot. "It's quite all right," said Wyckoff when he awoke, explaining that his fireproofed shirts, half asbestos, had been specially made for him by the firm of Charvet in Paris and would fully recover after a trip to the laundry. With that admission, they joined the ladies.

Old Knickerbockers

Sidney Dillon Ripley's immediate family was tightly wound into the gracious mid-Manhattan upper-crust world of a century ago. The family house was at 48 West 52nd Street, along which horse-drawn hansom cabs clip-clopped and milk wagons made morning deliveries to well-staffed households. The cops on the beat directed traffic, knew everybody, and got Christmas tips and presents. Dillon Ripley's father, the stockbroker and real estate entrepreneur Louis Arthur Dillon Ripley, proudly possessed one of the neighborhood's first automobiles, an 1898 Renault open tourer with solid rubber tires and wooden-spoked wheels. He drove the car with bone-jarring abandon through enormous potholes.

Ripley had detailed memories of his early years, as recorded in the extensive Smithsonian oral history interviews. His was a boyhood that in many respects foreshadowed the sort of man he would become. The young Ripley manifested endless curiosity and enthusiasm, a sense of wonder and excitement and humor. He inherited the upper-crust Anglophile speech habits and sometimes stuffy ways of his family. But he often also displayed a keen and very American interest in doing informal and unpretentious things. His childhood experiences gave him a taste both for elegance and for adventure, and indelibly endowed him with a deep interest in art as well as animals. He liked having living creatures around him and affectionately described their behavior in many of his writings.

Even when he was very small, Ripley was often taken by carriage to New York's Metropolitan Museum of Art. From its spacious front steps, he recalled watching the annual spring parade of the Ringling Brothers circus headed down Fifth Avenue toward Madison Square Garden. Once he was delighted to have been sprayed by a passing elephant and whisked back home to be scrubbed. He liked the Bronx Zoo, where once he experienced the "delicious excitement of the thrill of being charged by a galloping rhinoceros" and "imagining myself scared to death" even though a fence protected him.[3] Periodically there were excursions to the FAO Schwarz toy store, where, foreshadowing what was to be a life of frequent interest in travels, he was drawn to the electric trains. When he was about three, his father gave him one that circled on a track. At the time it was his proudest possession.

His received his first formal education at the Montessori Kindergarten School on Madison Avenue. This experience, he said, "was a very important formative element in my own education and made me forever interested in looking, feeling, examining, and handling objects, as distinct from merely reading about them."[4] He worked hard at solving the school's puzzles and completing his schoolwork, learned to tie his shoes, made models of Plasticine, and enjoyed using his hands as prescribed by the Montessori Method. The dexterity he developed helped him overcome the psychological barrier he might have harbored as a result of being unfashionably ambidextrous.

Early Travels in Style

During the summer of 1917, now four years old, Ripley embarked on a family trip to visit his Canadian mother's relatives in rural British Columbia. He found it a spectacular experience because it was his first encounter with open space. Though not yet generally interested in birds, he did sight a nesting pair of golden eagles, which were rumored to raid the farm's chicken house from time to time. It was doubtful that an eagle could get airborne holding a plump hen in each talon, but Ripley was fascinated by the very thought. During that visit, he put his own tactile inclinations to the test when he crawled under the house, picked up a sleepy rattlesnake, and, somehow remaining unbitten, proudly showed it to Miss Abernathy, his horrified Scottish nurse. On the way home by train via Montreal, he came down with a severe form of infectious typhoid fever, arriving virtually unconscious and with a raging fever, and almost died. He remained sick and recuperating all winter in a Providence, Rhode Island clinic. Doctors there managed to pull the young boy through after six months of severe illness, with liberal doses of homeopathic medicines and good food.

After recovering, Ripley returned to New York, but not for long. His mother was weary of her husband, from whom she had become increasingly estranged during the war. She was ready to leave bitter memories behind and dropped him entirely in 1918. Ripley was left with vague recollections of his father. His siblings and his mother were his principal sources of emotional support. Money did not seem to have been a problem. In April 1918, the family moved to Cambridge, Massachusetts, and rented a house off Brattle Street near Harvard. Ripley celebrated the end of World War I aboard a new tricycle circling round and round on the porch of that house.

In 1919, the family moved again, to 173 Beacon Street in Boston. Ripley was sent to the Noble and Greenough day school, which he disliked because as an outsider he was bullied by fellow students. He was shy and sickly, got colds easily, and passed an unhappy year there.

Later, Ripley was transferred to a suburban school called Rivers. En route by bus to and from that school, Ripley had long talks with his only real friend, the bus driver, to whom he felt very close, "about life as we saw it along the fenway, with ducks flying, and the stream, and a kind of simulated wildlife in the park-like stretches between Boston and the school." The school's headmaster subscribed to the idea that "the students should be virtually out of doors the entire year round" and adjusted the windows accordingly. Each student was equipped with an electric blanket that warmed things up a little. Somehow the fresh air agreed with the fragile Ripley. He missed his father, whose name was never mentioned by his mother or sisters, but was too shy to ask where he was. "I would invent the somewhat nostalgic, sad, and sentimental things about his being abandoned somewhere and having a sad life," Ripley recalled. "This haunted me for years until later I came into contact with him at the time of World War II" and learned something of what he was really like: a "bald and jolly little man, healthy looking, charming and amusing and great fun." Later there were various brief encounters, but never a reconciliation.[5]

During summers, the family made frequent trips to the family estate in Litchfield, Connecticut, aboard the train or a large green Cadillac touring car. Like many cars of the time, it often had flat tires that were hard to fix. For a child, recalled Ripley, the hazards made the trip a great adventure.

The cavernous family house in Litchfield, called Kilvarock, had been completed in 1905, with features borrowed from country styles in Britain, Europe, and Scotland. It had what Ripley called "slight overtones of a castle" with secret passageways and "endless vistas of nooks and crannies, and dark and mysterious corners, and out of which goblins would obviously pop in the evening."[6] For a young child it offered ample opportunity for exploration and hide and seek. As Ripley grew older, he said, the "special and mysterious quality" of the house added to its charm and fascination. It burned to the ground in 1976 and was never replaced, for want of insurance.

When he was ten, Ripley got his first taste of European travel with his family. His mother had decided to leave Boston and return to New York, but to delay the move to allow time for prolonged visits to several European capitals. For a while they rented an apartment in Paris. There Ripley maneuvered the model sailboats in the Tuileries pond. From to time he visited the adjacent Louvre to take in the art, and especially the Italian paintings. His mother had lost twelve Scottish relatives during World War I, and though she was an enthusiastic traveler, she never again wanted to visit Germany. While on their extended European sojourn, they visited abbeys, cathedrals, and castles in London, northern England, and Scotland. They feasted on pastries in Vienna and sampled Italy's culinary and artistic delights before returning to the States brimming with images of nature and culture.

In September 1924, Ripley was shipped off to the Fay School in Southborough, Massachusetts, twenty miles west of Boston, a boarding school for young boys. There he was once again hazed. "I remember," he said, "that we would be lined up with our faces to the wall of the outside of the building, and icy snowballs thrown at us by the older boys, who terrorized us in the dorms and made us feel very inferior indeed."[7] But he adjusted, coming to like some extracurricular activities such as singing in the choir, making extensive use of the library, and learning to play a decent game of golf. He fenced and rowed, even though he was not particularly gifted as an athlete. Signaling yet another emerging interest, Ripley played the role of gravedigger in a musical version of *Hamlet*. He enjoyed the experience and, overall, the school.

Sampling the World of Birds

At Fay, on weekend mornings in the spring, some of the students would get up early to go on bird walks with the rector of the Episcopal church in Southborough that they attended. This was Ripley's first real association with birds, in his eleventh and twelfth years. Seeing warblers pass through the churchyard in great profusion, especially near the spruce trees in the cemetery, provided a "marvelous vista of the spring migration." It "left an indelible impression on me, and I suppose started me off on my interest in birds," he said.[8] He was interested enough to join the bird club, chairing a committee charged with cleaning and watering a birdbath on the campus. He also welcomed the strenuous three- or four-mile marches that students were compelled to take, toting wooden guns, in order to work off demerits for infractions of the rules.

He never did graduate from Fay. Instead, in September 1926, at age thirteen, he was entered at St. Paul's in Concord, New Hampshire, a prominent entry among the cluster of private boarding high schools scattered across the New England landscape, as a first former (seventh grader). It was a place that ran like clockwork. In command was an austere rector named Dr.

Samuel S. Drury, who was a strict disciplinarian. He terrified most of the boys' parents. But Ripley's arrival at the school revealed a soft spot in the curmudgeon's soul when he let his new student's young life take a bold and unorthodox turn.

That summer in Litchfield, the Ripleys had gotten to know a young couple, John and Celestine Mott, who were about to depart for India. John Mott's father, having made a fortune selling a waxy coating to preserve some kinds of cheese, went on to found the Young Men's Christian Association. He won a Nobel Peace Prize in 1946 in honor of this effort to establish an international religious brotherhood. The young Motts, who were planning to found a YMCA hostel in India, suggested that the Ripley family come out and visit once they got settled. As it evolved, the idea would be for the three older Ripley children to go to California in October 1926, travel by ocean liner from there to Japan and China, then continue on to India, where the family would gather. His sisters were both done with their finishing schools, recalled Ripley, and older brother Louis was "on the loose." The only remaining obstacle was to get young Dillon sprung from St. Paul's as of the Christmas vacation and for the rest of the school year.

If permission for him to leave St. Paul's was granted, he and his mother would in December travel separately to Europe, across the Mediterranean to Egypt, then continue on to India, where the family would spend the rest of the winter and summer with the Motts and see the sights. "What do you think about it, children?" asked Mrs. Ripley. "At which point," recalled young Dillon, "we all chortled and chorused or clapped, or whatever it was that we did to say, yes, yes." Ripley played all the angles, saying, "The great tension in my mind was how could I possibly be included in such a magnificent trip?"[9]

In October Ripley's mother went to Concord to discuss
the matter with Dr. Drury, who had previously met young
Ripley at a lecture on Italian art that the stern headmaster
had given at the Fay School. Now he and Ripley's mother had
a long conversation, during which Ripley waited outside and
tried to remain calm. Drury and his mother emerged from
the rector's study. "Yes," she whispered, "you can go." Said
Drury, "I think that Dillon should go because he seems to
be so interested in making observations wherever he is. I was
fascinated by his ability to identify all the Italian paintings
in the lecture . . . and obviously travel would do him just as
much, if not more, good as staying here."[10] So Mrs. Ripley,
calling this adventure a "life experience," dipped freely into
capital to pay for it.

Posh Adventures Early On

In October she sent the daughters and older son off on their
separate visit to Japan and China. After school shut down for
Christmas vacation, she embarked with young Dillon on a
French steamer from New York for the first leg of their long
trip. Ripley had made solemn promises to keep up with his
St. Paul's homework. After sampling Paris and renewing ties
with cousins who lived there, mother and son went to Mar-
seilles by train, boarded a P&O liner, the *Mantua*, for a rough
winter passage to Port Said, and continued on to Cairo for
a brief stay at the old, grand Shepheard's Hotel. They visited the Pyramids, spent several weeks camping in the des-
ert under the care of an elegant dragoman (guide), and rode
white racing camels with a smooth gait. The party, all wearing
pith helmets to deflect the midday sun, mounted tiny donkeys

and rode them sidesaddle to get close looks at the temples of Luxor and Karnak. Along the way they encountered a snake charmer, who displayed no reaction when a large scorpion bit him. All this was great fun for a thirteen-year-old, said Ripley.

During their ten-day voyage aboard another P&O liner bound for Bombay from Port Said, mother and son were amazed by the ignorance about the United Sates displayed by their fellow passengers, of whom many were stuffy "caste-conscious" British civil servants. Always fond of dressing up and playacting, Ripley amused many of them by donning a dragoman's outfit for the ship's costume night and humoring passengers with "patter about come and have a camel ride with me and so on." At last they made it to Bombay, were greeted by the Motts and sent directly to the Victorian/Gothic Taj Mahal Hotel. It was, said Ripley, "the most romantic, straight out of Kipling hotel that you could possibly imagine." Donning their pith helmets once again ("I still have mine," said Ripley) and otherwise equipped for roughing it, they sampled the city's street life and were thrilled. Then, satisfying their habitual desire to know how the first half lives, he and his mother visited an old schoolmate of hers, who had married a member of the industrial Tata family and lived with him in grand style in a "splendid, gothic, Indianate marble palace."[11]

Driving up Malabar Hill on their way to the horse races, the family had a firsthand look at a famous incident of the time, straight out of Kipling and worthy of recording in family memory books. Said Ripley: "It was noticed that an automobile was racing up the hill at an extraordinary pace. . . . It was followed closely by another automobile, which finally edged it off the road into the ditch, at which point about six burly Indians armed with daggers leaped out of the following car, surrounded the first car, and attempted to stab a man and a woman who were inside. The woman was white, the man was Indian. During the melee, the assailants' death imminent, four British men aboard an open touring car, on their way to play golf at a nearby course, stopped gallantly, jumped out, whipped out their golf clubs, and beat off the attackers, rescuing this woman, who turned out to be French, and her Indian lover."[12] The episode, involving the Maharaja of Indore, eventually resulted in his being forced from his throne.

The story had a sequel, which involved the Ripley party firsthand after they had reached Kashmir and were living aboard houseboats. Standing on the roof of an adjacent vessel, anchored nearby, was a group of young men in dinner jackets sipping champagne. All then "proceeded solemnly to jump off the boat into the canal." They were "flushed and excited and screaming with laughter," Ripley reported. Invited to board the Ripley boat and have tea, they explained that they were the very same brave golfers who had intervened on Malabar Hill and "made a vow that they would spend their summer vacation in Kashmir and drink a bottle of champagne and jump in the lake. So that was that."[13]

Before reaching Kashmir, Ripley and his mother undertook the three-day rail journey northeastward across to Calcutta. There mother and son greeted the three other siblings at the conclusion of their separate transpacific journey. They ventured out in the Hooghly River to welcome the new arrivals, young Dillon swarming up the ladder to the deck of the big ship, proudly wearing his new Indian tailored clothes and sporting a cane that, said Ripley, was "totally unnecessary but made me feel very grown up."[14]

Invited to join a hunting party, Ripley's brother made himself famous by shooting and killing a tiger, a species then so commonplace that one maharaja had made his name by dispatching 1,050 of them. "There were thought to be an endless supply of those animals," Ripley reflected. "They were just a sporting object to shoot at, like shooting wild boar in Tennessee."[15] The maharaja gave a dinner party to celebrate the tiger shoot; there was a parade of elephants, and all the guests rode on them. Ripley's brother regarded the event as one of his life's great moments. Dillon recalled the wanton killing when, in Bombay in 1968, he gave a speech predicting that the species would be extinct in twenty-five years.

The family visited various sites near Calcutta, including the resort town of Nagpur, where they adopted a colonialist lifestyle featuring sports and exercise at odd hours, trencherman bacon-and-egg breakfasts, and boiled dinners. After a two-week stay, the local governor gave them a black-tie farewell dinner announced by footmen blowing silver trumpets. Seated below the salt, as British colonials called a low-ranking position at the dinner table, the Americans found the event "very stiff and very formal, and very old-fashioned." It was a far cry from "pulsating, intensely crowded" Benares on the Ganges, where a curious Ripley saw a large number of "largely undressed" people bathing in the river. The sight "aroused my prurient interests," he admitted.[16]

Then the party moved on to Delhi for several visits interrupted by side trips to celebrated towns with long histories of battles between ruling Hindus and invading Muslim Moguls from the north, and the great remaining legacy of fortresses, palaces, and castles. Near Agra they saw the Taj Mahal in the moonlight while wandering in its sumptuous gardens. Ripley made a good time exposure of the scene with his little Kodak

camera. Here and elsewhere in India, he displayed a keen interest both in photography and in another art form that would
resurface later: architecture.

In Udaipur, the party saw elephants trained to fight, butt-
ing heads and pulling each other back and forth with their
trunks, but not lethally. In Darjeeling in January, it was cold
and they had a clear view of Mount Everest. Continuing
northward, they visited Lahore and Rawalpindi and then Pe-
shawar and then in very cold weather traversed the Khyber
Pass into Kashmir, negotiating muddy and rough roads. In
Srinagar, Kashmir's capital, Ripley recalled, "we had a whole
family of Kashmirian people who looked after us—cook, butler, paddlers, assistants, laundry ladies or laundry men." With
Colonel Biddulph, an Anglo-Indian resident who lived aboard
a houseboat, they flew falcons. They fished for trout in fast-
flowing streams. And on one excursion, Ripley had an experience that would guide his later judgment at the Smithsonian
and in Litchfield about the role of gardens in large spaces. He
recalled that they

> picnicked over at the Shalimar gardens, which were Mughal
> gardens that had been designed on the shores of the Dal lake
> in the seventeenth century, and which are famed for the Shali-
> mar poem of an English poet and there's a song, a very roman-
> tic song, about "how I met my love in the Shalimar gardens."
> The gardens were beautiful, all running down the hills . . .
> over stone inclined faces, [and] the water glissaded down the
> inclined stones. . . . The channels were kept dry a great deal of
> the time, and they cultivated forget-me-nots in the channels,
> and then the water ran over them. When the fountains were
> running you saw those little forget-me-not faces under the
> water. It was the most charming idea . . . to plant the flowers
> in the bed which would be under water when the fountains

ran or dry when they didn't run. Pale hands I love beside the something, that's the part of the song or poem . . . pale hands beneath the Shalimar.[17]

As summer approached, the son and daughters pressed their mother to extend the adventure by continuing on from Kashmir and traversing the mountain passes to visit the remote kingdom in western Tibet called Ladakh. It had been conquered by the British but, said Ripley, getting there was arduous: it "was so inhospitable a country that only really Tibetans lived there."[18] A system had been established that allowed a maximum of twelve foreigners to trek in during the brief summer season when the route was navigable. The Ripleys, wait-listed by the resident commissioner, eventually secured two spots that had opened up. They conferred about which of them would go and eventually agreed that young Dillon and Constance, the younger of his two older sisters, would undertake the march.

Outfitting ensued, involving many trips to the market to acquire sturdy clothes, including leggings, jackets made of the light but warm wool called pashmina, heavy tweed jackets, and deerskin snowshoes, which, when broken in, enabled one to "walk endlessly" across the snowfields. Food, tents, cots, and sleeping bags were loaded onto some twenty-five yaks, whose food the pack animals also had to carry. All went well on twelve daily treks of up to thirty-two miles during which they staggered through deep snow, reaching altitudes of up to 14,500 feet en route to Leh, the capital and principal town of Ladakh. The little party remained healthy, although at one point Constance Ripley's small horse reared up when a gust of wind ruffled the onion-skin pages of a book she was reading while riding, Thomas Hardy's *Jude the Obscure*. The animal's

saddle girth broke, the whole saddle slid back, and the rider
was pitched off the rear end of her steed, uncomfortably but
not seriously injuring her back when she crashed onto a stony
pathway.

After buying supplies in Leh, the party continued on to a
town called Isis, where there was a famous monastery. There
they witnessed a three-day spring ceremony, an event held
only once every twenty-one years. This black-hat pageant, a
highly important dance in Tibetan monasteries, said Ripley,
"celebrates the triumph of good over evil and the banishing
of evil spirits." On the third day, they witnessed a rarely performed dance acting out the ritual killing and dismemberment
of the abbot of the monastery. Ripley watched the whole business and noted that the monks "appeared to be enjoying it."
After the show, all hands quaffed long drafts of the local bar-
ley brew to the tune of "loud brays" from fourteen-foot-long
trumpets, as small ponies and large mastiff-like dogs raced
along the streets of the town.[19]

During the fourteen-day return trek from Ladakh, along
narrow and sometimes scary pathways, Ripley fell victim to
an extreme case of dysentery, so severe that at one point some
thought he had died. Sister Julie, waiting below, got wind of
this and, borrowing a steed, dashed off from her camp wearing high heels, trotting and galloping up the trail to find the
afflicted Dillon. Reunited after this false alarm, the Ripleys
continued back to Kashmir to spend the months of June and
July there. They were surrounded by wildlife and natural
beauty. But, Dillon admitted, he did not recall being particularly interested in the region's birds or its natural history. He
was more interested in the game animals, he said — the sheep
and ibex that his brother was hunting.

Back in Bombay, the family boarded a small Lloyd Tries-tino steamer and undertook a stormy journey across the Indian Ocean to the Red Sea, during which one passenger on deck fell, broke his neck, slid from one end of the vessel to the other, died, and was buried at sea. Then, switching to the *Berengaria*, a large Cunarder, Ripley himself ignored the rules by venturing out in rough weather during the Atlantic crossing and was nearly washed overboard. His fourteenth birthday came up during the voyage. That day he was briefly reduced to bitter tears when he felt neglected at the thought that the family and the ship's banqueting crew had overlooked this event. But later in the day the event was elaborately celebrated, with emotions running high when Ripley admitted his adventure on deck.

That fall he returned to St. Paul's and the routines of boarding school life. He "must have been rather tedious," he said, as he regaled schoolmates with tales about his adventures in distant lands, but found them to be enthusiastic and friendly. He attacked his schoolwork, starting from the bottom of his class with much catching up to do. He wrote essays and poems for the school magazine. He debated, acted in some plays, and used public speaking to get over being shy. He helped found what was called the Offal Eating Club to harvest and consume road-killed pheasants, grouse, rabbits, and other game. He hurt his back in a football scrimmage and was compelled to give up the sport in favor of a brief fling with rowing.

Country Squiring at Home

Mostly, between St. Paul's and Litchfield, he lived the life of a junior-grade country gentleman. He frequently rode his sturdy horse, Patches, whose previous owner was the actor Rudolph Valentino, straight through to the outset of World War II. The family staged an annual horse show on the Litch-field property. Ripley fox-hunted, was "quite horse-struck," and wrote a principal paper at school on England's Grand National Steeplechase. "I must have been mad about fox hunting and polo and steeplechasing," he said.[20] There were cows on the farm and a profusion of vegetables. Ripley raised his own pheasants and enjoyed early-morning bird walks with schoolmates.

At the top of his to-do list, he placed tending to his ducks and their habitat on the family land. He said he could not remember when he had not been interested in small streams and the possibility of making ponds. His parents had once dammed a stream on the property and created a small pond, but as Ripley advanced through his teenage years, the dam had been destroyed. During the summer of 1930, with help from a team of horses, several schoolmates, and two family employees, a farmer named Toni Baldi and Mr. Kelly, an elderly squatter, he succeeded in damming the stream once again. Ripley's mother chipped in, giving him two pairs of pinioned ducks, two blue-winged teals, and two redheads to launch his collection.

Watching and minding these ducks soon became a passion, taking up "every waking hour that I could spare." By the time he went off to college in 1932, he had built a "real pond" on the property. A flotilla of eleven ducks of various species "swam about in the glory of their autumn raiment, vying with the beauty of the turning leaves," he wrote in his book *A Paddling of Ducks*. "I could not wait to return again as soon as possible to drink in the beauty and fascination of the pond."[21]

With the Depression and family financial losses, the Ripleys had to postpone further international travel adventures and remain closer to home during Dillon Ripley's upper-school years at St. Paul's. He resumed the early-morning bird walks that he had enjoyed at the Fay School. They became "the joy of my life," especially when he had the company of close friends. As graduation and college application season grew closer, he began to suspect he might need college training that would enable him to earn a more secure living than duck breeding was likely to provide. The law seemed a better choice for Ripley, who shouldered the idea with encouragement from his mother and brother, though he dreaded the drudgery involved.

Once again, at another critical moment, he sought advice from Dr. Drury, St. Paul's rector, who told him, "There's only one law school to go to, and that [is] Harvard." But, Drury added, if Ripley went to Harvard as an undergraduate, he would "disappear into the library and never be seen again. I think you should go to Yale because there you'll surely learn to slap people on the back."[22] So, dutifully, his future undecided, Dillon Ripley headed for New Haven.

CHAPTER TWO

Birds of Many Feathers

S tudent Plane Plunges into River as Entire Crew Squad Watches," ran a headline in an April 1935 issue of the *Yale Daily News.* The paper featured ads promising "excellent shooting" at a Millbrook, New York, hunting preserve owned and operated by Yale men, and plugged berths available for Atlantic cruises aboard the well-equipped schooner *Wander Bird.* To be sure, reported the Yale historian Rollin G. Osterweis, the Great Depression had affected some students, who "quietly dropped out of college to take jobs, in order to assist families once wealthy and now reduced to straitened circumstances."[1] A plaintive May 1936 ad offered for sale a $2,400 British sports car a student had purchased only ten days before, newly available "because of family objections." Overall, despite such evidence of hardship, the Yale of the 1930s remained a comfortable place, not greatly affected by the surrounding travails of the Depression era.

Most of the university's students, including Dillon Ripley, lived day to day in a comfortable bubble, largely oblivious to events beyond the campus. Most of them occupied suites in spanking-new residential colleges, patterned after English models, that were the handsome gift of the Harkness family. "No educational institution in the world could boast a more magnificent physical plant than Yale possessed by the close of the thirties," Osterweis continued.[2] One could document this appraisal with mention of the Sterling Memorial Library, the Law School Quadrangle, the Graduate School, the Payne Whitney Gymnasium, the Divinity School, and the enlarged Medical School, in addition to the undergraduate "colleges."

With Prohibition over in 1933 and New York State's drinking age set at eighteen, Yale undergraduates flocked to New York City watering holes such as the "21" club, formerly a speakeasy. For the Junior Prom those who didn't own them rented white ties, tails, and top hats. Custom tailors—J. Press, Langrock's, Fenn-Feinstein—were nationally known for their lines of men's hats and haberdashery. Students sported raccoon overcoats at football games. Cole Porter supplied the music and lyrics. Though a few students were offered scholarships, most did not need them and got along on family money. On the roster, composed almost exclusively of white males, were many who would later become famous: the Supreme Court justice Potter Stewart, the author John Hersey, the antitrust lawyer William Orrick, the historian Thomas Mendenhall, the elegant cultural leader August Heckscher, Ripley himself, and many other prominent future stars.

Approaching Science Hill

Yale students attended lectures by prominent scholars such as the literature professor Chauncey Brewster Tinker and the historian Samuel Flagg Bemis. Toward the sciences, said the *Yale Daily News*, they displayed apathy. A course critique handbook of the time advised undergraduates that a "gut" (easy) Introduction to Chemistry course was "a great way to pass off the science requirement" without making the long eastward trip out Prospect Street onto Science Hill, where labs and science classrooms were—and still are—clustered. When he was a Yale undergraduate, Ripley admitted, "there were sharp distinctions among the faculty and the administration between scientists and historians." In the latter group were most of the dominating intellectuals of the time. Scientists "were few and far lower in the peck order. My friends in the younger faculty or in my college (we lived in colleges, residence halls, each with a Master in the British fashion) hardly ever included scientists among their friends. Science courses were somewhat of a 'drag' except for those swotting to become doctors."[3] Academically, Ripley's choices followed those fashions rather than his emerging interest in biology. He roomed with the stylish August Heckscher and waltzed in New York and Boston, his sense of humor and his taste for high style often on display. He wrote a paper on Hitler's rise and became interested in foreign affairs, international economic development, and comparative literature.

Ripley's marks were not impressive. In his freshman year he averaged seventy-six and scored only eighty in biology, his top grade. He did little better the following year. Much later he explained that one year he had nearly flunked biology because he actively disliked the teacher, and he fared far better in humanities courses. Despite mixed results and continuing uncertainty about his academic goals, he added, his interest in scholarship had been stirred by the cum laude ranking he had achieved at St. Paul's School, as well as by an essay prize he had won. Despite appearances, he claimed, he had studied "very, very hard" as a Yale undergraduate and had no excuses to offer for his lackluster performance. "I'd had my ups and downs," he explained. "The educational process of absorbing information comes in cycles." The record found in the Smithsonian Archives indicates that Ripley may have been interested in some of what he studied, but his overall academic effort during his "bright college years" as a Yale undergraduate seems not to have won him much more than a gentleman's C.

Though not known for athletic prowess, he made the fencing team, as he had at boarding school. He rowed and played tennis and golf. And he acted. He played Phileas Fogg in a Yale Dramatic Association production of *Around the World in 80 Days* and according to one critic did "amazingly" well. He earned formal recognition of his own status as a drama critic for the undergraduate-run *Yale Daily News*. He thought of trying theater as a career and reviewed some plays. Thanks largely to his restless mother, he was already an experienced traveler and considered applying to the Foreign Service. Over Sunday lunch in Litchfield, his mother gave a copy of a short story he had written to the Yale-educated writer and editor Croswell Bowen. In a five-page letter to Ripley, he pronounced it an "excellent piece" and suggested possible publishers. Though that initiative led nowhere, Ripley's nonfiction work later appeared in several widely circulated publications.

As an undergraduate, Ripley had treated birds with casual interest, finding informal ways to study them. "At Yale I did other things," he wrote. "The study of birds had been a hobby."[4] Even though the field of ornithology hardly existed in the Yale of those times, Ripley found opportunities to exercise his quietly growing interest in birds outside the classroom. A taxidermist at Yale's Peabody Museum of Natural History taught him a skill that would become of central importance to his work: how to skin and mount birds felled in the field for their incorporation into museum collections. Occasionally, he said, he looked at the museum's exhibits. He also visited the American Museum of Natural History in New York, examined bird skins, and met the bird curator Ernst Mayr, a pioneer in the emerging field of evolutionary biology, who would become a lifelong friend and mentor. The ornithologist Frank Chapman, a well-known writer of field guides also at the American Museum, taught Ripley the basics of bird collecting and classification. As a sophomore he had tea with the eminent German ornithologist Erwin Stresemann, whose thoughts and writings were to help awaken his interest in ecology. Ripley especially enjoyed wandering in the woods to study birds, and especially ducks and geese, and devoting many hours to the care and feeding of the waterfowl collection he had established in Litchfield — merely an hour away from New Haven.

While still an undergraduate, often in the company of his boarding school friend Hugh Birckhead and his cousin Wolcott Ripley, Ripley did much to build and diversify this collection. Well fed, many of the Litchfield birds became tame and tugged at Ripley's shoelaces in search of extra rations. After ending their sophomore year in May 1934, he and Birckhead and Henry Hoyt, another school friend, headed way down east along the rocky coast of Maine on a trip to harvest eggs from eiders, a common Bay of Fundy sea duck species, and take them to Litchfield. The eggs would travel in style, in a well-padded light blue Tiffany's gift box provided by Ripley's mother. The precious cargo arrived at Litchfield at 2:30 AM to be placed underneath broody Rhode Island Red hens. Mortality was high, but before long the pond's collection included two large eiders that were "handsome" and "sleek."

This was only the first of many eider experiences for Ripley. "Since then I have found it hard to be without those quaint and handsome creatures, so tame, so full of character, and so beautiful," he said.[5]

The Fateful Decision

Ever more as his interest in birds grew, Ripley was manifesting a complacent attitude toward his family's Depression-era concerns and a determination to make his own way in the world rather than serve family business interests. Thus inclined, Ripley during his senior year at Yale made his fateful career decision to bypass history and the law and become an ornithologist. He did not like to see birds sit or perch below the salt, he said, where their needs often became "regrettably subordinate" to those of humans.[6] His mother encouraged him. "Why, of course," she said, "that's exactly what you should do."

After graduating from Yale in the star-studded Class of 1936, he with some reluctance moved to New York. Acting on Ernst Mayr's advice that "the most important thing you can do is get a sound and broad biological training," he enrolled at Columbia University, initially taking, one by one, the science courses that were prerequisites for earning a doctorate in his chosen field. They bored him. "I really wanted to go into ornithology," he wrote. But he faced "the dreary prospect of four or more years of study in alien subjects without any experience or background to give me some perspective, or hope. I was caught up in chemistry and genetics, enmeshed in histology and anatomy, all of which seemed very far away from birds."[7] Moreover, he disliked city life and "would much rather have stayed at Litchfield, taking care of the ducks, or else gone off somewhere to look at birds." This was, he concluded, "the subject I was most overwhelmingly interested in." But he realized that he "would have to work hard at graduate study to pick up the scientific courses which [he] had missed in New Haven," and settled in to the task.[8]

In the fall of 1936, once Ripley had done enough classroom work for the American Museum of Natural History's Ernst Mayr to rate him as an ornithologist of sorts, there arrived in the mail a surprise proposal. The letter, sent at the Heckscher family's suggestion, was from the anthropologist Charis Denison Crockett, a member of a well-off Philadelphia family and a friend of the Heckschers. She and her husband Fred, she wrote, had acquired a handsome fifty-nine-foot schooner, the *Chiva*, and were planning "to sail out to Dutch New Guinea and spend a year or more cruising around the coast and small islands nearby. The Academy of Natural Sciences of Philadelphia is very interested in the idea and wants us to make bird collections for them. We need a zoologist and wonder if you would care to go" on what became known as the Denison-Crockett Expedition.[9]

It was a piece of "sheer luck," said Ripley. He hastened to ask around about how to respond, making a beeline for New York's Natural History Museum. "You cannot get to New Guinea every day," advised Ernst Mayr, who had himself explored some of the South Pacific islands. "Graduate work will still be waiting when you come back and then, too, you will be better prepared for it."[10] Ripley learned that New Guinea had some six hundred species of birds, none of which he had ever seen in the wild, and with alacrity he followed Mayr's advice.

That fall, in preparation for the expedition, Ripley studied with Mayr his latest research and that of Germany's Erwin Stresemann. In the footsteps of Darwin and Alfred Russel Wallace, these pioneer scientists had highlighted the importance of making observations in nature rather than in the lab. Studies of the proliferation or disappearance of bird species in remote locations might serve as keys to a broader understanding of how they survived in small-scale environments without the "endless niches" available to those inhabiting a large continental area. Analyzing these trends might affect scientific understanding of the principles of island biogeography, and of evolution itself. Ripley regarded this as "one of the most fertile ways of stimulating the imagination."[11] His initial New Guinea adventure would mark only the beginning of a lifelong fascination with the subject and lead toward his long and close association with the eminent Evelyn Hutchinson, a distinguished Yale professor since the 1920s and a pioneer ecologist.

Off on a Boat

On December 1, 1936, saluted by a small dockside crowd of well-wishers, *Chiva*, a classic yacht designed by the blue-chip John Alden firm, set forth down the Delaware River from Philadelphia. The crew consisted of the Crocketts, Charis Crockett's Bryn Mawr College roommate, a navigator, an engineer, and a cook. Ripley's subsequent South Pacific adventures, and the story of his evolution as a passionate bird lover and skilled field biologist, are richly described in his spirited book about the expedition, *Trail of the Money Bird*.

All did not go smoothly on the 12,000-mile, ten-month passage to New Guinea. Along the US Atlantic coast, *Chiva* ran hard aground in the shallow intercoastal waterway along the Atlantic shoreline and braved stormy weather off Cape Hatteras. The boat's balky and rusty diesel engine conked out in the Panama Canal, a tricky section of which had to be navigated under sail. At one point Ripley slipped while mopping a muddy patch of deck, was left "hanging head down between the canal lock's wall and the boat," and almost saw unexpected service as a "human bolster." Near the Galapagos Islands a pet parrot, "such a friendly brave little thing," as Ripley put it, fell overboard and disappeared. In Tahiti, where a weeklong layover had been planned, it was discovered that the boat's entire stern was, said Ripley, "soft and pudgy with dry rot."[12] Mandatory retimbering took an unscheduled three months, until June 28. A further delay in Rabaul, New Britain, for bottom repainting and replenishment, set the expedition back another three weeks. Ripley birded while waiting for the boat and crew to be readied for the 450-mile westward passage to New Guinea.

Hiking the Bird's Head

On September 28, 1937, *Chiva*'s crew at last sighted what was then called Dutch New Guinea, a wild and mysterious tropical place of sixteen-thousand-foot mountain peaks and verdant valleys, torrential rainfalls, and a profusion of endemic wildlife, including fifty-two species of spectacular birds of paradise. These were of special interest to Malay traders, who for centuries had cruised the region, but few outsiders ventured far inland from the coast, which remained the domain of Papuan tribespeople with their own languages and customs.

That autumn and winter, Ripley and various shipmates

cruised around and near the remote "Bird's Head" on the
northwestern end of the large island, bigger than any on earth
other than Greenland, little explored by scientists from anywhere. *Chiva* carried Ripley much of the way. After the boat
departed from the region to be sold in Manila, he and the
Crocketts continued to explore the island on foot and aboard
small craft and *Ursula*, a motor vessel commanded by Mr. van
der Goot, a mostly Papuan who served as the Dutch colonial
magistrate for the region. He was a master at the skills needed
to get along with edgy local people. Bird collecting continued
at a steady pace.

After Christmas 1937, Charis and Fred Crockett installed
themselves in an inland village called Sainkedoek in order to
conduct anthropological studies. Ripley and his crew, whose
members included Mr. van der Goot and a resourceful fac-
totum called Jusup, trekked separately through often inhospitable terrain, visiting a succession of small communities in
search of birds and other wildlife. Besides many species of
paradise birds, Ripley encountered odd specimens such as the
beaked giant echidna, which looked like a "walking pincush-
ion," said Ripley, and ranked as New Guinea's strangest animal. Bivouacs were primitive, and food was sometimes scarce.

A small number of Papuans along with ethnic Malays occupied coastal settlements in the region, some Christianized or
exposed to the larger world through trading. Others lived as
roving itinerants in isolated upland areas, little if at all visited
by outsiders, where a small dispute or violation of tribal cultural values could still erupt and become fatal. In dealing with
these sensitive people, caution and diplomacy were required.
In this very region, as recently as 1936, mountain tribespeople had overpowered and killed a German backpacker
named Schacht.

Herr Schacht had mistakenly lost his temper with a group of tribal people at a critical moment while hiking in a highland area near Ripley's route. Tribespeople there had little contact with the coast and were, van der Goot said, "known to be cannibals." "Not wanting to have any individual responsibility," the magistrate continued, "they sharpened a stake and all leaned on it until it went through him. And that was the end of Schacht," who was left uneaten because the community felt that their white victim would harbor a very strong and unpalatable ghost.[13]

Elsewhere in the mountains of the Bird's Head, Ripley encountered what he described as a "very matter of fact" attitude toward cannibalism. In a village called Wejos, the *kapala* (community leader) told Ripley that there was a food shortage. "It is a hard thing," he said. "But I think we should kill one of our children." That outcome was averted when the community decided instead to kill and eat something of equal value: a large pig of the sort that local women would breast-feed along with their own progeny. A feast ensued. Ripley chipped in tobacco, and the group started to dance, the celebrants "chanting out their strange dirges and swinging around in a circle, arms locked, eyes glassy, almost hypnotized by their own rhythm." Pig blood and lime smeared on them, the young children performed the same initiation rituals they would have had one of them been killed.[14]

In several villages Ripley and his shipmates were thrilled to observe entire communities erupt into this sort of celebratory dancing. But they had to take care to avoid having misfortunes blamed on them, van der Goot advised. Ripley was not in the business of handing out medicines. But were he to do so and the patient continued to suffer, the magistrate counseled, he had assumed responsibility and could end up being roasted. In

1919, a butterfly collector had entered the region, waving a net around. The Papuans thought he was crazy and dangerous, and dispatched him. To avoid danger, the Ripley party needed to be careful about getting too close to the Papuans at delicate moments, as when they wanted to observe a recently deceased man being smoked over an open fire. Said a local host in one community, "You must always remember not to make these people afraid of you unless you are in a safe position."[15]

In one upriver canoe trip, Ripley engaged in a spirited series of campfire discussions about cannibalism with his hired paddlers. They were quite accustomed to eating human flesh, reported Ripley, perhaps to make up for a chronic protein deficiency in their diet, and unhesitatingly listed their favored cuts (arms, legs, babies roasted whole). Parts of the corpse deemed unhealthy would be buried, not eaten. The paddlers were loath to discuss the subject only because of Dutch regulations banning the practice, but Ripley was able to get them to talk quite openly about the details. As salty Europeans, the Ripleys were relatively safe since the Papuans "disliked strangers or foreigners" and preferred to eat parts of somebody they knew. In one area, "if someone dies in the family the relatives ceremonially eat a little piece of that person so they will have a souvenir, a memory for the rest of their lives."[16]

Ripley recruited dozens of Malay "boys" to carry heavy loads of food and gear along muddy and slippery mountain trails to primitive campsites. He trained especially gifted ones to work as cooks or waiters. It was rough going. Ripley dispatched an eleven-foot python in his sleeping quarters (it was quickly cooked and eaten by the porters) and climbed a tree to elude a nasty wild pig. The hiking party faced torrential tropical cloudbursts, slippery narrow pathways, occasional tidal waves, two kinds of leeches, particularly unpleasant nettles, severe food shortages in isolated villages, malaria, and downright cold weather at the higher altitudes of the mountainous island. Ripley suffered from a festering broken blister rubbing on his boot that became a "rough red spot the size of a half dollar," severely inhibiting foot travel. During one notably arduous side trip, Ripley surfed perilous, reef-strewn waters aboard an outrigger canoe (*prahu*) crewed by expert paddlers. Booted feet were seldom dry. While visiting a scruffy coastal port called Sorong, Ripley asked the captain of the government mail boat if he had ever been ashore there. "Good God no," spluttered the Dutchman. "I never go ashore in these filthy places."[17]

The wonders of the captivating birds in this "virtually terra incognita" region, where Ripley followed in the footsteps of such illustrious nineteenth-century adventurers as Darwin's colleague Alfred Russel Wallace, made up for all the hardships. There were brilliantly colored forest parrots and gnarly cassowaries, crowned pigeons and brightly hued cockatoos, rare bat-hawks and noisy hornbills, scarlet parakeets, herons, ducks, and kingfishers. Some could be found only on or near the coast. Others remained at higher altitudes. Almost everywhere there were birds of paradise; the males of these birds, some quite small, display colorful erectile plumes to attract mates.

Finding the Money Bird

Ripley was particularly attracted to a species known to Malays as the "money bird," which he called the "king" of the paradise birds. Money birds are "beautiful little things about the size of a starling. The head and back on the male are bright glossy red, the bill is milky blue, and underparts are white. From the rump two narrow wirelike feathers are prolonged out over the short tail for four or five inches. At their ends they curl tightly and flare out into two shining disks of metallic green." The remarkable bower bird, which Ripley called "a dull colored cousin of the paradise birds," has a special talent. It builds a little house for its mate, then decorates a front-porch dancing area with flowers, pieces of fruit, or other small oddments. Having observed a number of bower birdhouses, Ripley suggested a "phylogenetic" succession in which evolution carried the birds toward ever more complex housing arrangements.[18]

Gunning down and skinning examples of these and other species was Ripley's principal mission, and he worked hard to fulfill it, training his dexterous helper Jusuf as well as some Malay "coolies" to help with the task. "Preparing birds is an intricate job which takes a definite amount of learning," he wrote.

> The skin of a small bird is delicate and easily torn. Rough treatment means that many feathers can be lost. All the innards of a bird are removed except the skull and some of the wing bones. The skin is then padded out with a cotton or excelsior manikin in the shape of the body, a small amount of arsenic powder is dusted in to keep out insects, and the skin is sewed up and wrapped away in cotton to dry. When completed, a museum or study skin looks quite unlifelike, rather as if the bird had just lain down on its back, folding its wings neatly underneath and crossing its legs. A tag is then tied to the legs giving the data of place, date, sex, and so on, and the skin is complete.[19]

As if it weren't difficult enough to do the skinning right under comfortable circumstances, Ripley and his helpers often had to work at sea with pitching decks or at poorly equipped camps out in the field.

In April 1938, Ripley arrived once again at the port town of Sorong. There his mother was awaiting him. She had pledged to help Ripley bring back his treasures, which by now included thousands of bird skins plus eighty-seven live birds in forty-two cages demanding regular feedings of fish, bananas, papayas, and other perishables not well suited for a tropical climate. Aboard a succession of ships, via the Indonesian ports of Makassar and Surabaya and then Singapore, this odd assortment made its way around the Cape of Good Hope and eventually, after a forty-nine-day passage, to Boston aboard a small Dutch freighter called the *Talisse*. Thanks to skillful and attentive ministrations by Ripley and his mother, all but a few of the birds survived. When they finally reached Boston on July 14, it was cold and drizzly. Said Constance Baillie Ripley, "I shouldn't mind at all just turning around and sailing somewhere else."[20]

"As we split open the fruit for the last time on the boat," Ripley wrote, "the parrots did aerial evolutions on their perches, the bright crimson king bird of paradise leaped from bar to bar of his cage with the speed of a winking light, the ducks pattered up and down in their box, the storks jabbed, the herons stabbed. . . . We were home at last, and the long, perilous trip was over."[21]

On his arrival home from New Guinea, in the summer of 1938, Ripley made haste to deploy his birds. Most of the skins went to the Philadelphia Academy of Natural Sciences, which had sponsored the Denison-Crockett Expedition. Some filled long-standing gaps in museum and zoo collections. A rare pair of pygmy owls from Biak Island replaced the last example collected by anyone: a single male that had been acquired in 1875 by Italians and deposited at the Natural History Museum in Genoa. Some of the live birds would eventually be given or sold to the Philadelphia or Bronx Zoo or to dealers. Some were given to friends. One duck stayed at Litchfield along with a salmon-crested cockatoo from the Molucca islands. Ripley would happily have stayed home with his collection for a while, but separation from his ducks was once again inevitable as he shuttled between the Philadelphia Academy, the American Museum of Natural History in New York, and the Smithsonian on various internships and unpaid research assignments.

Back to Asia

In February 1939, Ripley departed on a second bird-collecting trip to Asia at the request of the Philadelphia Academy of Natural Sciences. His skipper this time was George Washington Vanderbilt, a St. Paul's School classmate who had already spent several years helping the Philadelphia Academy build its flora and fauna collections. The destination was the rugged, little-explored, mountainous backcountry of Aceh Province at the northern end of Sumatra. This was a jumbo three-hundred-coolie effort described in the local Sumatran newspaper and mentioned in letters by John Ketcham, the nearest local US consul general, as a party as "sumptuous . . . as an imperial cartage at the time of the Roman Caesars" that became a "continuous tale of woe."[22]

Vanderbilt's wife, Louise, along for the ride, took sick. So did her husband. Ripley suffered from "heavy" malaria. Passports and money were lost when a truck stalled and skidded into a muddy river. Coolies pilfered supplies. Vanderbilt harshly criticized Ripley, who traveled separately for some portions of the expedition and diverged from the planned itinerary in order to photograph war dances of tribespeople on remote Nias Island off Sumatra's west coast. Vanderbilt accused Ripley of having compiled what he felt was a "pretty terrible record" on collecting bird specimens, disobeying instructions, and lacking "even the decency to send us a note explaining your strange movements." He charged Ripley with having "absolutely no regard for my schedule, you waste days in nearly birdless territory, cost me a hell of a lot of money, but don't help the collection to any great extent."[23]

For all the backbiting and rumormongering, Ripley described the expedition's results as having exceeded all expectations, with a thousand specimens in hand, including many "new" species. The Philadelphia Academy's bird curator, Rodolphe Meyer de Schauensee, a widely admired specialist on tropical birds who had anonymously underwritten the Denison-Crockett Expedition to New Guinea, expressed admiration, calling Vanderbilt's a "splendid collection." En route home in 1939, Ripley and the expedition's mammal expert, Fred Ulmer, had a good laugh when confronting officious Japanese authorities. In Hong Kong they had boarded a Japanese steamer, the *Tatsuta Maru*, whose crew grew hostile to foreign passengers as war approached. Ulmer had brought aboard two mammals, a gibbon and a binturong from Sumatra. As the steamer approached Japan, a ship's doctor "menacingly" invited Ripley and Ulmer to produce stool specimens "immediately" in test tubes as an anticholera measure. Noting that the gibbon's cage had not been cleaned, Ripley surreptitiously harvested and presented gibbon stool for inspection. Ulmer worried, but Ripley never heard again from the ship's medical officials.[24]

Home Again as War Clouds Darken

In 1939, Ripley remained in touch with some worldly and sophisticated Japanese ornithologists, who offered amusing side notes as war clouds darkened. He was becoming increasingly worried about Japan's overall behavior in the region, and he sensed big troubles ahead. As he said much later:

> In 1938 and '39 the Japanese, having occupied most of China, were already on the move in southern Asia and the islands. Travelling and living in Indonesia, Singapore, and the China coast one could sense it in their often rude manner, their tendency to be authoritative and brusque if military, and even the cockiness of civilians, quite different from Japanese I had met or known in the world of science. Whatever natural preoccupations one might have with the war in Europe and the dangers there for everyone, it would be foolish indeed to overlook the menace lying behind our backs. The long sweep of history should teach one to have premonitions. Those who walk in the woods mark the trail behind as well as forward. But once aroused to the peril and the horrors in Europe, the sense of imminent danger to us all in the west became curiously concentrated, blinding one to a broader perspective of signs and portents outside the immediate horizon.[25]

In 1938, while they were docked at a New Guinea town called Manokwari, Ripley and *Chiva*'s crew, sleeping on deck, experienced a taste of what politically lay ahead. A hum turned into a drone as four twin-engine Dornier flying boats roared low across the town, then headed out to sea. Then, dwarfed by the "long, squat shape of a big cruiser, rose the conning towers of three submarines. In toward us over the waters of the bay churned six longboats manned by white-clad sailors and marines. They drove past us with a rush. Whistles blew and the figures jumped out and ran at the double up the shore with fixed bayonets."[26]

By one count, Japan's mock capture of Manokwari had taken twenty-two minutes. The Japanese sweep across the Pacific would not, it seemed, take much longer.

CHAPTER THREE

Asian and Other Adventures

B ack in the northeastern United States early in 1940 after completing his Vanderbilt odyssey, Ripley spent some time as a volunteer helping Rodolphe Meyer de Schauensee organize his newly expanded Sumatran bird collection at the Philadelphia Academy. Ripley was professionally at a crossroads. Under his belt he had several years of field and research experience centering on the Far East, but he still "lacked the academic standing that would qualify him for regular museum work or teaching."[1] But while the coming war would further impede his progress toward an orderly academic career, it would also showcase the breadth and depth of his talents.

In 1940, he once again enrolled in graduate school, at Harvard this time, and began seriously to make up courses and research for his biology doctorate "before the emerging world war overtook us all." He won a Harvard fellowship, as an anonymous gift from the Museum of Comparative Zoology's director, Thomas Barbour, to take the required courses and work on his doctoral dissertation (on the birds of northwestern Sumatra). Ripley completed all the coursework by the end of 1941. "The orals day came and went," he wrote. "Dry-mouthed, I managed to survive, having flubbed only one question from an embryologist about differences in embryonic development of bone and cartilage, a relatively simple question which I insisted in my own mind on making complicated, and so became mired in quicksand to the professor's delight."[2]

After Japan's Pearl Harbor attack on December 7, 1941, Ripley joined many other graduate students in facing a future that, he wrote, was "clouded with doubt and uncertainty. It was almost impossible to be consumed in one's own studies . . . in that welter of buffeting news from all sides of disasters to the east and to the west."[3] Jobs for junior ornithologists were scarce even as the economy was gathering steam for the war effort. It was not possible to organize research expeditions. Relocating his Litchfield ducks to the safety of the Bronx Zoo in New York City, he therefore tried for a US naval intelligence commission.

Ripley thought that his by now extensive Asian experience could somehow be helpful to the war's conduct. Having been in the Pacific for most of the previous five years and become fluent in the Malay language, he felt comfortable in the East Indies, which were "as familiar to me as my own home." Naval intelligence beckoned as a way for Ripley to apply that intimate knowledge of the region to the war effort. But thanks to his extensive travel in the backlands, he had become pencil-thin, devastating malaria attacks having dropped his weight down to 170 pounds on his scrawny, nearly six-foot-four frame when he underwent a physical examination. He was declared unfit even for deskbound military work in the light of what he felt were cumbersome peacetime health requirements for military service.

Off to War in Washington

As he sought some other way to participate in the war, luck and guidance from well-placed mentors once again intervened. When Harvard's Museum of Comparative Zoology convened the midwinter 1941–42 meeting of its high-level Visiting Committee, scholars gathered from near and far. One participant was Alexander Wetmore, assistant secretary for science at the Smithsonian and the nation's top-ranking ornithologist of his time. Introduced to Ripley, the gently courteous Wetmore said he had recently suffered a death in his department and wondered if Ripley might be interested in becoming the new assistant curator of birds. Ripley accepted this "manna from heaven" with no hesitation and was soon on his way to Washington with a dual mandate.[4] He would undertake his first real job, as assistant curator of birds, at what is now called the National Museum of Natural History. He would also make use of the extensive but insufficiently studied Smithsonian collection in completing his doctoral dissertation on western Sumatran birds.

His first day at work was a snowy March 10, 1942. The museum's entryway was a formal place in those times, he wrote, with new brassy elevators "presided over by elegantly uniformed ladies" serenely sporting highly starched handkerchiefs projecting from their left breast pockets. Once inside, Ripley found himself amid a cluttered array of offices and storage spaces for specimens. "Offices led off the corridor, their doors sunk into the space between the cases like concealed embrasures for archers or other castle defenders, or assassins lurking behind the arras in some ancient palace."[5]

Stationed in an office near the Department of Entomology, which occupied space adjacent to the bird division, he got a good sense of its scientists' research methods while "running the gauntlet" past their chemical-laden quarters. "I could never tell who might creep or crawl or pounce out of those recessed doors, always seemingly shut until an inhabitant came out," he wrote. He occasionally encountered a lady entomologist with a gimpy leg who "swung her cane briskly against the legs of passers-by," and avoided a white-haired fly expert who "possessed an inescapable and overpowering smell." Another door remained always closed, causing Ripley to wonder if someday the cleaning staff would "force their way in, only to find the shriveled remains of Mr. Somebody bent over his desk, brown paper bag lunch and thermos bottle beside him[.] I never found out." Said the former Smithsonian secretary Leonard Carmichael in a heavy whisper as he pointed Ripley toward a shadowy figure scuttling toward the doorway to the Great Hall, "Look. That was a curator." It struck Ripley as a strange observation, a confirmation of his impression of the atmosphere as "Edwardian, if not Victorian."[6]

Ripley's own lightly furnished office, all steel and government-issue green linoleum, was equipped with a brass spittoon, which was kept brightly polished in honor of a departed user. Escaping occasionally to the Mall's art museums along with his boss, the bird curator and art historian Herbert Friedmann, he enjoyed studying fourteenth-century Renaissance paintings and medieval manuscripts, "which often had fascinating marginalia pictures of recognizable birds, insects, or flowers" and "told one something of the history of the knowledge of natural history." As spring blossomed, Ripley moved into a spare bedroom of the Friedmann house in northwest Washington, an arrangement that gave him a coveted free ride into work. He enjoyed "a modicum of social life, mostly with senior curatorial staff or intellectual colleagues." Humor was lacking, he continued, and the engrossed scientists paid scant attention to the pleasures of the adjacent art offerings. The Friedmanns "had brought together the most stimulating and eclectic company of which the Smithsonian was then capable," said Ripley, and he made do.[7] He left later in the spring to move into the home of the art- and music-loving lawyer Walter Bruce Howe and his family, friends from New York and St. Paul's School, to share in their cultural life.

An Unlikely Spook

By June 1942, with his doctoral thesis nearing completion, Ripley also established links with Washington's intelligence community, such as it was. As late as 1941, said the senior diplomat Robert Murphy, US intelligence operations had remained "primitive and inadequate . . . timid, parochial, and operating strictly in the tradition of the Spanish–American War."[8] Many activists were pushing a reluctant President Franklin Delano Roosevelt to become better prepared for war and to develop better intelligence-gathering capabilities as part of an effort to protect US security interests. In this regard Roosevelt came to rely heavily on the energetic and entrepreneurial General "Wild Bill" Donovan, a World War I Medal of Honor winner, to sort things out. Roosevelt tapped Donovan to be coordinator of information (COI), a civilian position attached to the White House, with a mission to gather intelligence and advise the president on national security issues. Without delay Donovan added clandestine espionage and other undercover activities to the tasks, and what started as a White House position soon became an agency. In 1942, it was retitled the Office of Strategic Services (OSS). Quickly this upstart agency gained the attention of leading citizens, Ripley among others, seeking ways to combat Nazism more vigorously.

A large number of prominent Yale faculty members and recent graduates had responded to calls from the OSS. For Ripley, encouragement and access to Donovan came via the extensive network of Yale-groomed intelligence advisers and officials populating the OSS, including the ebullient and witty historian Sherman "Buffalo" Kent, for whom Ripley wrote some research materials. The millionaire Yale trustee and Walpole scholar Wilmarth S. "Lefty" Lewis, who also had joined the OSS early on, was Ripley's link to Donovan's office. Later there came a steady procession of OSS-bound Yale graduates and professors. Some poked fun at Yale's British dining club brand of espionage as described by the historian Robin Winks in his book *Cloak and Gown*. A reviewer, Godfrey Hodgson, likened the gentlemanly Yale version to a cozy British scenario: "The port goes around, the fire blazes merrily on the grate, and old Winks has the floor."[9] No fewer than forty-two members of Yale's class of 1943 signed up, reported the *Yale Daily News*.

Initially, Ripley "informally" did part-time research while "on loan" from the Smithsonian to COI's Asian division. His first assignment was to prepare a pamphlet on the birds of the South Pacific, and he found the work stimulating:

> I doted on recalling the rain forests and high mountain moss forests of New Guinea and Sumatra, recalling to my mind's eye exotic birds of paradise, hornbills and pheasants as I pored

over war maps of territory that I had walked over, hearing again calls of megapodes or cockatoos, and cries of gibbons, high-pitched songs of the jungle. What a foretaste of my own work during the war of which I then had no premonition.[10]

Invited to join Donovan's COI staff full time as of June 13, 1942, Ripley was asked to resign from his Smithsonian curatorship. It irritated him that the Smithsonian refused to keep his chair warm for him during his wartime absence. He made it clear, though, that this reduction of his esteem for the Institution did not extend to several of its scientists. He maintained contact with Friedmann, Wetmore, and several others he had come to know and admire. He also found time to express frustration about the shabby treatment the Smithsonian accorded the magnificent artworks that had been donated to the nation by the reticent Andrew Mellon. Support for displaying this art was "so meager, so dusty, so lacking in demonstration . . . of interest on the part of a poverty-stricken self-absorbed group of semi-barbarians." Ripley's concerns also had to do with "faltering administration, declining budgets, pitiful salaries and indifference to the outer world." He could hardly imagine ever returning there. "So much for the Smithsonian," he said. "After the war I will head back north to a more accustomed clime and look for work in New York or New England."[11] Little did he know what lay ahead.

At COI, Ripley initially served as General Donovan's liaison to the British espionage team called British Security Coordination (BSC) under Sir William Stephenson as "passport control officer," which was clustered at Rockefeller Center in New York (a position held after the war by this author's father, Patrick W. Stone, a retired Royal Navy commander). BSC's mission was to improve Anglo-American cooperation in the intelligence field, offset Nazi propaganda, and help Roosevelt promote the war effort.[12] Ripley stayed aboard when COI was retitled the Office of Strategic Services in July 1942 and given expanded espionage responsibilities. Not for personal glory but because he saw needs not being addressed, Ripley said he quickly "became swept up in the enthusiasm and dedication of wartime research and planning."[13]

For a short time Ripley was slotted for research in the OSS's economics section, on rubber, quinine, and other strategically important commodities. But OSS administrators soon became persuaded that Ripley's talents would be better used if he shifted to the secret intelligence branch of the OSS and oriented his work toward Southeast Asia. This switch compelled him to undergo rigorous OSS training at the secret field station in western Maryland that later became the presidential retreat called Camp David. There, in the company of a mixed bag of recruits, including some with criminal records and a professional wrestler from Manila, he was exposed to a variety of extreme black-arts techniques. While he could manage a ".38 sawed-off magnum Colt revolver in my waistband and pull it with ease," he proved himself less handy with other weapons. He was "positively squeamish about carrying a tiny, extra-sharp knife in a soft suede leather pouch posterior to one's own natural male pouch" and "totally incapable of effectively performing silent death techniques because I couldn't really carry through after the first provocative gesture." His instructor was a rough-hewn British ex-commando named Major Fairbairn, with whom he had extended and animated conversations. The wiry major, who "could garrote a man as soon as look at him," said Ripley, rightly concluded that Ripley would never have the will to maim or gouge an antagonist "to the end."

The derring-do of a James Bond was not for me. In life there is a subtle difference perhaps in not fearing shells, bombs, explosion, or gunfire, and yet being uncertain of one's ability to push through some mental barrier to kill an individual in combat. To me it seems to require more than courage or indifference to the fear of death, but rather the surmounting of an invisible hurdle, forfeiting intellectual perception. Later on, under fire or behind the lines, I never felt that firing a gun was a problem but I did feel, if I thought about it all, that I could not go through with it to the end in physical contact. At least I never had to face the problem.[14]

After his camp experience, Ripley found life back at OSS headquarters to be rather humdrum. In Washington he did, however, learn something of the intrigue and inter-service rivalries within the intelligence community, involving the FBI, the OSS, the navy, and other military branches. The backbiting made him wonder about the number of lives lost thanks to actions taken by jealous principals. As a "new boy on the block," the OSS was "particularly suspect" and wrongly thought by many in the Allied Commands to be yet another intelligence agency aimed at building "a new wave of Neo-Imperialism" under an expansion-minded American Eagle. To his dismay, Ripley then and later was to find British and other European contacts simply assuming that in the postwar reshuffling they would be the ones to get back their colonial enclaves.[15]

Ripley also developed great respect for many of his OSS colleagues working on Southeast Asia, and resented accusations that they were more socially inclined than substantively effective. "The sobriquet 'oh so social' for OSS and some of its members," he said, could better be described as a kind of "cover" mechanism for many of the staff, who were later to risk their lives many times over in foreign operations. I thought of them more as Scarlet Pimpernels, covering their troubles with a quip and a joke or some phrase of self-disparagement. Blowing one's trumpet was not the oss style.[16]

Back to Asia

In June 1943, Donovan selected Ripley to join General Douglas MacArthur's Australia headquarters as oss representative. Ripley was awarded an "assimilated rank" of lieutenant colonel to claim prisoner-of-war status if captured. Ordered to fly to Australia via Egypt, India, and Ceylon, he stopped in London and spent ten days there. He was billeted at Claridge's. Entering the building, he was elbowed aside by the doorman, "resplendent in top hat and gilded capelet over his stout full coachman's coat, calling out loudly, 'make way for his Grice, the Duke of Sutherland,' in a manner bespeaking the style of linkboys and postilions rather than the smattering of taxis that might appear." At the hotel he dined on whale meat and soggy boiled vegetables served with what Ripley called "great aplomb and dash" by the well-trained staff. Ripley lunched with his first oss boss, David Bruce, brother-in-law of Paul Mellon, at Bruce's "delightfully cozy and removed small townhouse in a mews behind Grosvenor Square," rented from the polo player Tommy Hitchcock. And of course, Ripley visited the bird collections stored at the British Museum of Natural History.[17]

He briefly joined Donovan in Morocco, after a perilous flight during which his plane came under fire from a German submarine while crossing the Bay of Biscay and "rocked about a great deal."[18] The party stayed at the Mamounia in Marrakesh, the famed haunt of Winston Churchill's. Then Ripley moved on to Cairo, where he enjoyed an "exuberant" lifestyle, recruited a few OSS agents, and had a memorable visit with the US ambassador, Buffy Kirk, a Yale man out of another era. Ripley described him as "overwhelmingly distinguished, wearing an 'orchidee' silk suit with a pastel mauve tie in which was fixed a large gray pearl stickpin, and with gray suede shoes."[19] Tongue firmly planted in cheek, he discussed Ambassador Kirk's efforts to cement US relations with Saudi Arabia.

Kirk had, he told Ripley, enjoyed a marvelous visit with Emir Ibn Saud in Riyadh. Upon reboarding his DC-3 plane for the return flight to Cairo, the ambassador had discovered that its rear cabin was "simply stuffed" with gazelles. Diplomatically unable to refuse this gift from the Arabian royals, Kirk after landing had consigned the "adorable creatures" to Cairo's zoo. There, kneeling while eating, they had developed sores on their legs that became infected. Several had died. "What shall I do for my dear little gazelles?" asked the ambassador at lunch. Ripley "took a deep breath" and then, not able to resist mimicking the ambassador's style and mannerisms, trilled deadpan. He felt confident, he said, that Hermès in Paris could make "dear little knee pads to measure, in beige suede." For a small additional surcharge, Ripley added, Hermès could even "add your initials in darker suede." The suggestion went over well, and the party enjoyed a splendid luncheon.[20]

Ripley never did make it to Australia, for want of official clearance from the self-absorbed MacArthur staff. "MacArthur would brook no possibility of interference from Washington," Ripley wrote, "certainly not from a novice organization of non-regular persons who had a tenuous link to the White House."[21] Barred from continuing on to Australia, Ripley pressed on instead from Egypt to China, India, and Ceylon. In India, as a ranking OSS officer, he tried to work the OSS into Lord Mountbatten's British army units planning to sabotage Japanese-held properties in the former Dutch East Indies.

Continuing on to the OSS encampment at Szemao in southern China, he was named secret intelligence officer for OSS Detachment 404, covering Southeast Asia, and instructed to set up a clandestine OSS station at a town called Kandy in Ceylon's central highlands to which Mountbatten had relocated his Southeast Asia Command (SEAC) headquarters. Though rated an unimportant "gilded birdman" by some British officers in the region, Ripley got along well with most of them (including the Allied Southeast Asia commander, Mountbatten) and with China-based US military and OSS units. He worked with some success to smooth the often prickly relations between the OSS chief, Donovan, Anglophobic US military leaders in southern China, and the British in India. He also managed during those years to squeeze in some stretches of bird fieldwork in India and Ceylon. By the time his assignment in Ceylon ended in 1945, perhaps exaggerating a bit, he claimed to have seen every species of bird on the island.

Part of 404's mission in the region was to support Allied efforts to curb Japanese offensives. Ripley's unit also sought to inhibit European efforts to restore colonialism after the war and instead to pave the way toward establishing independent democracies in Southeast Asia. At the tactical level, Ripley's Detachment 404 prepared agents for deployment behind Japanese lines, by foot, seaplane, parachute, or submarine, in Burma, Indochina, Indonesia, and Thailand. The detachment also struggled to set up clandestine radio links between oss stations and covert transmitting facilities, and infiltrate its own agents into underground units to bolster resistance efforts. While Ripley did not personally conduct the training and deployment of these units, it was his job to plan and organize them. Most of the missions undertaken in 1943 and 1944 failed: many oss-trained agents were successfully launched but were never heard from again. As the war approached its end, however, more fruitful times lay ahead for the oss in the region and for Ripley's 404.

Tiptoeing into Thailand

Thailand, the former Siam, was a special and important case. This exotic kingdom, familiar only to a handful of Americans, had never been conquered even after most of the region had become dominated by European colonial powers. When Japanese troops moved into Thailand on December 8, 1941, the day after Pearl Harbor, Japan was preparing to establish Thailand as a staging area for offensives against Malaya and Burma. American and British residents were interned. The premier, Field Marshal Phibun Songkhram, declared war against the United States. "Unless a way could be found to escape the embrace of Japan," said the historian E. Bruce Reynolds, "Thailand would go down in flames; perhaps even lose its treasured independence."[22] But as described in Reynolds's authoritative book, *Thailand's Secret War*, even as Japanese troops occupied much of the country and fifty thousand of them swarmed into Bangkok, the tide began to turn as the Japanese offensive lost some of its initial punch and Thai political support began to wane.

Free Thai movements had been formed in Washington and

London, with individuals—mostly college students from elite families—receiving training in anticipation of eventual paramilitary actions. Within Thailand an underground secretly backed by a powerful politician and Phibun's chief rival, Regent Pridi Phanomyong, took shape. More and more high-ranking officials, including the police chief and several government ministers, joined this anti-Japanese movement and became ever bolder in their subversive actions. What evolved, said Kermit Roosevelt in a postwar analysis, was "what might best be described as a patriotic governmental conspiracy against the Japanese in which most of the key figures of the state were involved."[23] Japanese naïveté helped. Said one Free Thai alumnus, Piya Chakkaphak: "Because of their feelings of superiority and their attitudes toward the Thai, the Japanese could never believe that the friendly Thai among whom they lived could be capable of such skillful subversion."[24]

Increasingly, as Thai military and police units quietly lined up behind Pridi, it became possible for OSS operatives, as well as some from Britain's Special Operations Executive, to be smuggled into Thailand and engage in espionage activities. An example: A Japanese inspection team was scheduled to fly into a clandestine airstrip secretly controlled by the United States. The OSS officer in charge, a Baltimore banker named Alex Griswold, simply walked away from the village, a Colette novel in hand, and remained out of sight as the delegation arrived and was served foul-looking water. When the Thais murmured something about cholera in the region, the Japanese hastily reboarded their plane and hurried off to the next stop.

American spies and Free Thai cohorts began setting up shop even in Bangkok under the noses of the official government. In early 1945, one Free Thai agent lunched almost daily with Japanese officers and that same afternoon reported what he learned over drinks with Major Howard Palmer of the oss, who was treated so well by the Thais that he gained fifteen pounds while living behind enemy lines in a series of royal palaces. oss operatives were also able to establish guerrilla outposts in dense forest areas that were patrolled only lightly by Japanese forces. Starting in March 1944, when Ripley and his colleague Fisher Howe established the 404 station at Kandy, he was a keen participant in the organization and management of multiple oss operations in Japanese-occupied Thailand. The OSS records supply ample information about operations in which Ripley was directly involved and also establishes him as a participant in many broader policy discussions at senior levels.

At first the Japanese and pro-Japanese Thai units detected and disrupted most of these activities, causing Ripley that November to send Washington gloomy reports about the failure of his group's infiltration initiatives. But as the war's end drew closer, things began looking brighter. After many frustrating months during which Free Thai agents within Thailand were not able to make radio contact with the outside world, a link was finally achieved on October 5, 1944. This feat caused jubilation at the oss station in Szemao, China, 650 miles away on the Laos–Burma border. Subsequently, technicians hidden in the heart of Bangkok began transmitting daily news reports. Regular radio communications ensued. Efforts to arm and train Free Thai units became ever more productive, and recruiting for the underground ever more successful.

The Pacific War officially ended on August 15, 1945, just after the first atomic bomb devastated Hiroshima. It remained unclear, though, whether Japanese troops in Southeast Asia—almost 1 million in number—would honor the Japanese emperor's order for them to lay down their arms. Seven thousand weapon-brandishing Japanese soldiers patrolled Bangkok's streets, and over fifty thousand more manned checkpoints elsewhere in the country, said Bob Bergin in *Studies in Intelligence*. Shooting continued in many parts of Southeast Asia. In view of the dangerous uncertainties, Mountbatten sent Ripley to Bangkok on an undercover visit to enhance the thin 404 presence there, undertake the exfiltration of prisoners of war, and, he wrote, satisfy his curiosity about "the state of mind of the Jap commander and his forces and their potentialities."[25] The OSS and Mountbatten, Ripley recalled, feared that they might not only continue the war from the mainland but also set up pockets of resistance where their troops were in occupation overseas.

Accordingly, Ripley undertook the most hazardous adventure of his OSS career. He packed tommy guns and pistols, as well as a rumpled dinner suit that, he said, would have to do if he was called upon to officiate at surrender ceremonies. Together with the OSS officer and naval lieutenant commander Ed Taylor, he boarded an aged Thai Air Force B-10 bomber, "the only one left that could still crawl through the air," for the audacious flight from an undercover airstrip at Pukio in northern Thailand to the partly Japanese controlled Don Muang Airport near Bangkok, where Thai forces controlled the one hangar from which the Japanese were excluded. "It was the first time that Americans had landed at Don Muang secretly in the daytime," Ripley said. He and Taylor remained hidden under blankets, weapons at the ready, as the plane taxied past groups of suspicious Japanese soldiers. Finally a "sleek black Buick," commandeered by "Dickey," a Thai air force colonel and ranking member of the underground, "slid into the hangar." Still fingering their weapons, the party drove through town toward its "official" area of palaces and broad avenues, ready to pass as neutral Danes or Swiss if challenged. They had to duck down again as they entered the Palace of the Roses, Pridi's former residence, which had been established as the oss headquarters in Bangkok, passing guards loyal to Pridi, who "had no idea what they were guarding" since they had been selected for being deaf and dumb.[26]

Once installed there, Ripley and Taylor were lavishly received and entertained by swarms of "ministers, gunmen, admirals, generals, agents—all came at any time from dawn to late at night." Ripley's two-week visit also featured copious banquets with ample food and drink, some provided by an underground member who also managed the city's best hotel, and dancing girls who, Ripley reported, were "very cuddly looking little things." The menu on his final black-tie night featured lobster Thermidor, goose with aromatic stuffing, shrimp soufflé, ice cream made with steamed bananas, and long formal toasts. A twenty-piece orchestra played "energetically," wrote Geoffrey Hellman, and Ripley executed a Siamese dance called a *ramwong* that Taylor described as "snaking around, waving your hands as well as your feet, not actually holding your partner."[27]

In between such events, Ripley and Taylor managed to negotiate and bring about the departure of all several hundred surviving Allied airmen who had been downed and interned in or near Bangkok. Working in cooperation with Thailand's pro-Western chief of police to get clearances, Ripley and his oss colleagues recruited a small squadron of Royal Air Force c-47 airplanes to airlift the prisoners out to India. For his leadership, Thailand later awarded Ripley the Order of the White Elephant, which he ranked highest among his career total of sixteen such decorations from as many countries. Ripley, continuing to live the life of Riley, stayed on in Bangkok until September 2, when he left to escort the Thai chiefs of staff out to India and Ceylon to meet Mountbatten, and then returned to Washington. The war in Thailand was coming to a spectacularly bloodless end.

None of these miracles could have happened were it not for Pridi's discreet and skillful maneuvering within and beyond the underground. At war's end, wrote Reynolds, Pridi's moves to ally many high-ranking government officials with the underground had "served Thailand well. He had obtained British and American sanction for a policy of maintaining relations with the Japanese while building up resistance forces with clandestine Allied support . . . the Allied response had spared the Thai the bloody task of fighting the Japanese army."[28] The story of the "secret war" in Thailand had been a remarkable chapter in OSS and espionage history, not fully known or appreciated until OSS records were finally declassified. The agency "was not just running intelligence agents who were part of a resistance movement, but dealing with the 'key figures of the state' on matters of great importance."[29]

While based in Kandy, Ripley had as usual taken advantage of opportunities to have fun. He shared many a meal with Julia McWilliams, later Julia Child, then also at the OSS. At that time, Ripley said, she "couldn't boil an egg." Other prominent "Kandy kids" were the anthropologist Gregory Bateson, who introduced Child to her future husband Paul Child, and Julia Child's roommate and OSS colleague Mary Livingston, who in 1949 would become Ripley's wife. Dillon Ripley enjoyed many a sundowner (afternoon refreshment) with nearby British tea planters. In New Delhi and the major naval base at Trincomalee on the island's northeast coast, he cultivated Mountbatten, whom, despite the United States' misgivings, he found to be great company as well as "decisive, intelligent, and effective" and a good companion at black-tie dinners to whom Ripley reported on guerrilla activities in northern Thailand.

Losing a Bath Towel

Amid all this, Ripley did not totally neglect his birds. Every spare moment that he could manage during his two years in Ceylon, he wrote in his book *A Paddling of Ducks*, he scoured Ceylon's magnificent and varied countryside to look for birds and collect specimens, using an elaborate kit that the Smithsonian's Alexander Wetmore had supplied. Along the way he encountered not only birds but also dangerous wild water buffalo and, once, a small herd of elephants, some "maliciously inclined" and "very fond of playing with and wrecking small cars." Fortunately, he was able to keep his jeep a safe distance from one he dodged, ready to "adopt any stratagem than have to shoot an elephant."[30]

He discovered a new subspecies of Ceylonese thrush. Ceylon's *Daily News* reported that, in 1945 alone, Ripley had sent the Smithsonian no fewer than 354 skins from the island, and a single bird skeleton as well. He tallied five hundred bird species in all. And Ceylon was where, in an often-repeated anecdote, Ripley clearly revealed his sartorial priorities. One afternoon, clad only in a towel, he was out with his shotgun collecting birds. In the tea bushes he gunned down a green woodpecker. As he hastened to retrieve the bird, the towel fell off, to the surprise of Mountbatten's nearby cocktail guests. That very bird rests to this day, a blackish-gray specimen of modest size, in a container at Washington's National Museum of Natural History. Carefully tagged, the bird carries this inscription in Ripley's handwriting: "Shot at cocktail party . . . towel fell off."

Upon completion of his Bangkok mission and at war's end, Ripley made haste to disengage himself from the OSS and return home. He was tired and needed a long vacation. His accomplishments had included not only his organization of clandestine activities but also his contributions to the broad policy debate about how to keep Southeast Asia out of postwar colonialists' hands as well as those of the Japanese aggressors. In 1944, when he was named Detachment 404's secret intelligence chief, his performance had already won kudos from Whitney Shepardson, the overall OSS intelligence director in Washington, who wrote: "We are highly pleased with all that you have done out there until now—both the things that require action and those that require finesse. We have every confidence for the future."[31] General Donovan added a warm note of commendation in a letter dated October 1, 1945, which in part read: "The Organization of Strategic Services was charged with the duty of carrying on irregular warfare in support of military operations. Both individually and as part of that organization you have made a fine contribution to the winning of this war."[32]

"Here we all were," reflected Ripley as he departed for Rangoon from Don Muang, his war service effectively over after his dangerous Bangkok sojourn. "American, British, French, and Dutch, in a British plane flying on Jap gas. Japan was still at war and would be for another week. . . . Siam was theoretically at war with Britain and America. Britain had declared war on Siam, but America had not done so. It all seemed very confusing. I gave it up and turned to look down on Siam, that small hemmed-in nation which had had so miraculous an escape."[33]

The record shows no indication of later contact between Ripley and the CIA, the successor of the OSS, except for one casual Vietnam War–era encounter when Ripley repeated to a CIA officer the commonplace recommendation that the United States get out. Ripley's service in Asia had branded him as not only a scientist or museum curator or professor, but a man of multiple talents. Praise was heaped upon him for skills he hardly knew he possessed: untiring efforts in planning and contributing to successful intelligence operations, his ability to make contacts and help other units, his imagination.

CHAPTER FOUR

Pleasantly Busy
in New Haven

In December 1945, soon after completing his scary Bangkok
mission, Ripley resigned from the OSS and returned to the
US Northeast. Exhausted, he took a long vacation. Then
he began looking for an academic post that would satisfy him
at home and also give him the elbow room he needed to build
on his already extensive scientific record in Asia and the South
Pacific. As it turned out, he was embarking on a long and
pleasant stretch of his life that would last for eighteen years,
from his 1946 appointment to the Yale faculty up to his 1964
departure from New Haven to take over the Smithsonian.

In 1946, Ripley got a job offer from Harvard but declined,
feeling that there he "would be a very small frog in a large
pond." The Smithsonian made an offer as well, wanting him
to come back as an associate curator. But Ripley wanted to be
in New England, closer to his family, who lived in Litchfield.
Yale was only an hour away. The university offered him a joint
appointment as a lecturer in zoology, with the rank of assistant
professor, and as an associate curator at the Peabody Museum.
He would divide his time between being a professor and museum administrator, doing science in the field, and being a
part-time country squire in Litchfield.

Yale would pay him at the scale of a lowly instructor. His wife-to-be, Mary Moncrieffe Livingston, complained that he did not care about money, although she thought he had good taste.[1] Exercising his customary bravado, he shrugged off this objection, accepting Yale's offer. Ripley's appointment was in part the result of a talk he had in 1946 with a board member of the Yale Corporation, "Lefty" Lewis, a powerful friend who had smoothed his pathway into the OSS. To Yale's curriculum planners, Lewis "pointed out that ornithology was not represented at the university at a graduate level, and that although the Peabody had a bird collection, it didn't have a full-time ornithologist." Lewis noted that Ripley was "exceptionally housebroken" and could help the Peabody's dinosaur experts establish closer relations with Yale College aesthetes and humanists who "move about in the great world."[2]

Once aboard Yale's faculty, Ripley rose steadily up its ranks. In 1949, he became an assistant professor of zoology. In 1951, he was named a curator at the Peabody. He won both a Fulbright fellowship (1950) and a prestigious Guggenheim (1954). After spending six years living abroad, he was contentedly putting down sturdy roots in Connecticut. In 1949, he married the formidable Mary Livingston, a New York–born divorcée he had met at a cocktail party in Shanghai while both were serving in the OSS. Impeccably blue-blooded, Mary Ripley also had credentials as an entomologist, an avid gardener, a geographer, a photographer, and a tireless traveler. Soon the couple had three daughters: Julie, born in 1951, Rosemary (1953), and Sylvia (1956). The burgeoning family lived in a roomy house, number 880 on New Haven's tree-lined Prospect Street, and spent many weekends and holidays in Litchfield.

The Peabody Years

At Yale in 1959, Ripley had already spent a dozen years as a professor, curator, and field scientist. A search for a new director at the Peabody Museum, a Yale faculty appointment, was under way. Ripley, by dint of his academic achievements and courtly demeanor, became an obvious candidate for the job. The historian A. Whitney Griswold, then Yale's president and a good friend, cautioned Ripley that the position would be "stuffy and dull" and advised him to turn down the offer. But, seeing the job as an opportunity to blend science and showmanship, Ripley said yes—and set about awakening Yale's old dinosaur of a natural history museum.

While there he detected a sense of inward-looking "muzziness," as he called it, about museums' self-esteem and avoidance of their great potential as educational as well as archival centers. Foreshadowing his subsequent performance at the Smithsonian, Ripley did much to polish the Peabody. He launched multiple outreach efforts. Following in the footsteps of his mother, who had been an active charter member of the women's committee at the Museum of Modern Art in New York, he founded a similar group in New Haven.

This initiative gradually grew into a lively Associates program featuring lectures, field trips, evening gatherings, tours to scenic sites, bird walks, and other activities. Soon it began to attract husbands. Membership reached one thousand before Ripley departed in 1964, having fully come to believe in the importance for museums of looking outward—even though it involves a lot of "fertilization and cultivation." It was here that Ripley formed his initial set of ideas about museums as educational centers, not just storehouses. Here, too, he became aware of the associates' potential as donors to the museum, remaining ever alert to income-generating opportunities.

He also booked for the Peabody an early mini-version of what would become the blockbuster King Tutankhamun exhibition of Egyptian treasures that was to captivate the nation late in the 1960s. The larger show won high praise and record crowds at such grand places as New York's Metropolitan Museum of Art and the National Gallery of Art in Washington. For Tut's preview in New Haven, Ripley took the controversial step of charging an admission fee. Throngs of visitors gladly forked over, forming waiting lines around the block for the first time in the Peabody's long history. To celebrate the event, he organized a dinner featuring alcoholic beverages — another first for the museum. A belly dancer performed, bursting into tears when some guests seemed not to appreciate her art. Mrs. Griswold is said to have danced on a dinner table. The evening was, said Ripley, a "wild success."

Teaching with Hutch

Intellectually, Ripley was experiencing a deepening preoccupation with ecology and disappearing species of plants and animals. This awareness came in large part thanks to his long association at Yale with a ranking pioneer in the field: G. Evelyn Hutchinson or "Hutch," as he was often called. He was becoming widely admired as no less than the father of modern ecology. Hutchinson viewed science as art and would raise searching ecological questions arising from his studies of water bugs and freshwater systems. He captivated generations of students and scientists whose work of whatever sort he found to be "profoundly interesting." He was a keen student of medieval animal art and taught a course with a jazz musician, reported his biographer, Nancy Slack.[3]

In her view Hutchinson was a polymath, a "rare scientist who bridged the two cultures, the scientific and the humanistic," and who "left little unexplored."[4] Too busy to pause long enough to earn a doctorate, he took pleasure in studying just about anything he could lay his hands on. His studies of water insects led him toward viewing biology as an entryway into his later work in ecological theory. He profoundly influenced the emerging disciplines of biogeochemistry and ecosystems ecology, arriving at Yale in 1928 and working there for sixty years, blending his important theoretical work with field studies such as the benchmark data he gathered as lead biologist on Yale's 1932 expedition to North India.

There developed a long and mutually rewarding relationship between the two men. Hutchinson became one of the mentors pushing Ripley toward a life in science and deepening his interest in the challenge, central to Hutchinson's work, of preserving the planet's biodiversity. They talked frequently. For eighteen Yale years, Ripley co-taught an ecology course with Hutchinson, concentrating on islands and island biogeography as "one of the most fertile ways of stimulating the imagination." Ripley had not done much fieldwork in ecology. But he had an impressive record of classic field experience, and Hutchinson

> liked that because his specialty was invertebrates and my specialty was vertebrates. He felt that we could talk and cover the waterfront a little bit to the graduate students, and that we could inspire them in different ways—he with his studies of lakes and aquatic invertebrates, and I with my studies of

terrestrial habitats in the tropics. Mine was rather anecdotal because I had lived in the field and studied animals. His was rather laboratory-bound because the bulk of his fieldwork had occurred many years before he came onto the faculty.[5]

Together they seemed to find ways to relate everything to everything else and to motivate a new generation of eager followers. Over the years their bumper crop of graduate students would do much to advance ecology as a new scientific field.

Generally, during his eighteen years as a Yale faculty member, Ripley was happy with his family and friends, his work, his life. It was a busy time. While curator of vertebrate zoology, he managed the bird collections at the museum, taught both undergraduate and graduate courses, was an active member of the Department of Biology, was an active member of advisory committees on architecture, architectural planning, and honorary degrees, and did exhaustive research on his own collections. He thought that he would stay at Yale for the rest of his career.

On the scientific side, Ripley encouraged another faculty awakening, setting an example with his own extensive fieldwork. The number of bird specimens collected by the Peabody Museum had drifted along for its first hundred years, peaking at about two thousand in 1920. According to a Peabody tabulation made the year after Ripley became director, the number started shooting up the year Ripley took over. It reached more than twelve thousand when his directorship peaked, and tailed off after he departed.

As a prolific writer himself, of popular as well as scientific books and articles, he cared especially about providing ways for curators and scientists to get their research results published and more widely appreciated. To this end he founded a low-budget journal called *Postilla* as a flexible new publishing outlet for professors, curators, and graduate students. Hundreds of issues of *Postilla* were produced during Ripley's time in office, and many scholars joined him in the belief that information had to get out without undue delay. "Let them have mistakes in them," said Ripley, "because then one's colleagues bother to read them and point out the mistakes," while flawless ones "go to sleep on the shelves."[6]

Travels with Ali and Others

While serving on the Yale faculty, Ripley also made time for arduous travel to collect and study birds. In negotiating the terms of his job in New Haven, Ripley had won a commitment from Yale that would allow him to spend half his time out in the field, studying and collecting birds. His archive contains detailed information about where he went, when, and why — often with Mary, sometimes with the children as well. He had many adventures in the least accessible parts of Asia and Africa. In 1948, he reached remote parts of Nepal, from which almost all foreigners had long been denied access, on an elaborate search for the Himalayan quail, last seen anywhere in 1876. He studied Darwin's observations in Ecuador's species-rich Galapagos Islands, finding information there to confirm his own thoughts about evolutionary biology. In photo sections of the Smithsonian archives, you find him as often riding an elephant as using more conventional means of transport, or wearing a sun helmet somewhere in the steaming tropics. His itineraries often included visits to world-class aviaries and waterfowl breeding stations manned by Sir Peter

Scott in Slimbridge, England, by Jean Delacour at Clères, France, and by the Duke of Bedford at Woburn Abbey, his celebrated nature park in the British countryside.

More and more, beginning in the late 1940s, Ripley underwent an intellectual transition from classic zoology to broader ecological concerns and the conservation of wildlife and wildlands. He wanted to study live birds—their movements and behavior—as well as dead ones.

These interests tightened his long-standing and productive partnership with the ecologist Sálim Ali. Born in Bombay in 1896, Ali was raised in privileged circumstances as a member of a prominent merchant family. As a child he became interested in birds, initially while gunning down sparrows with a BB gun, and found his way to Hornbill House, headquarters of the Bombay Natural History Society, a classically British colonial institution. In his book *Inventing Global Ecology*, the historian Michael Lewis describes Ali's determination to become an internationally certified ornithologist even without much formal training and having been rebuffed by colonialist scientists at the British Museum, where Ali said work conditions would have been uncongenial. He went on to Berlin, where he was welcomed by Erwin Stresemann, who would, said Lewis, become "one of the twentieth century's most famous ornithologists."[7] Stresemann, who had also spent some time at Yale and inspired some of its most influential zoologists, trained Ali in the new science of behavioral ecology. Even though they worked together for only seven months, the experience was sufficient to establish Ali as India's top-ranking ecologist. Ali never remarried after the premature death of his wife in 1939, and consecrated his life to studying birds.

During World War II, Ripley had worked hard to include

Bombay in the itinerary of as many of his frequent trips from Ceylon to India as possible. One purpose of these visits was to meet and get to know the highly respected Ali and to plan cooperative postwar fieldwork. Ali's *Book of Indian Birds*, a field guide, had established him as his country's equivalent of Roger Tory Peterson, the white-thatched, sharp-eyed American ornithologist who, in a series of field guides dating from the 1950s, introduced millions of Americans to the joys of birdwatching and made it a highly popular spectator sport. Ripley thus became aware of Ali's great charm and his tight focus on the life of birds.

The affinities between them led to a lifetime partnership. Each had chosen birds over business prosperity, and liked and respected the other. Soon after World War II ended, the diminutive Ali and the lanky Ripley established a Mutt-and-Jeff friendship that would last from 1946, when they made their first field trip together, to the state of Assam in northeastern India, until 1987, when they made their last one. Eventually, their collaboration would result in the joint publication of their classic work, the ten-volume *Handbook of the Birds of India and Pakistan*, thirty years in the making, which was first published in 1968. The massive *Handbook*, which Lewis called no less than a "masterpiece," covers "the taxonomy and ecology of every known bird species on the Indian subcontinent."[8] In a notable display of the multitasking Ripley's ability to set his own priorities, Ripley and Ali began the demanding task of writing the *Handbook* in 1964 — the very year that Ripley started work as the Smithsonian's secretary.

The Ripleys never minded roughing it or courting danger. In 1960, they spent three months in New Guinea. Leaving their daughters with a nanny in a provincial capital, they reached remote upriver areas (similar to those Ripley had visited in 1937 with the Crocketts), where they lived with isolated people "quite accustomed to eating human meat," a practice that provoked interesting discussions. "They had found and experimented with eating ... Europeans, which would include Americans or British, anything like that," said Ripley. But "they couldn't bear the meat because it was terribly salty," and they had no salt in their natural diet. Nor did the Papuans enjoy eating the occasional Japanese who landed among them during the war, complaining about their "horribly fishy" flavor. "I was never frightened of those people at all," Ripley later said,

> except in one case earlier in New Guinea where a poison fruit had been given me by a woman I saw. I was led to believe that for some reason or another she was perhaps trying to seek revenge for some episode in her family that might have happened where a white person ... had to her mind been involved in the death of a relative. .... At least that was a possibility. As they knew so few outsiders, so few foreigners, they assume we're all related, we're all one family of some kind.[9]

The Ripley party went on to climb as high as nine thousand feet into cold and wet weather, but with so many rare or little-known bird species to see or rediscover, Ripley was "anxious to go higher." As Mary Ripley demonstrated often during their many years of travel together to distant lands, she was surprisingly resourceful out in the backcountry. Wrote Sálim Ali: "She struck me as singularly unfit for the rough-and-tumble conditions she would have to face. However, after sharing several expeditions with the Dillon Ripleys subsequently, I realized how sadly I was mistaken: Mary Ripley, amid the elegance of her Washington drawing room, is not the same as Mary Ripley in safari outfit in a dripping leech-infested camp."[10] Winding up their summer of 1960 trip to New Guinea on schedule, the family made it back to New Haven in time for the three girls to start the academic year with their classmates at the private Foote School.

Detailed planning preceded Ripley's departures from New Haven, with Ripley listing needs down to the last yak or coolie. In this manner, for example, he arranged a trip with his wife to the remote Himalayan kingdom of Bhutan. Extensive correspondence traces the course of the expedition, whose purpose was to study bird migrations as well as to apply Smithsonian expertise to improving indoor lighting at the seventeenth-century Paro Museum in the capital city of Thimphu, then Bhutan's only museum. Letters and memos about logistics shuttled between there, Washington, and New Delhi. Reverent attention was paid to food and drink (forty-eight bottles of rum for the thirty- to forty-day trip), kerosene heating for the Ripleys and Sálim Ali's accompanying delegation of four in tented camps, and such esoterica as procuring heavy Bhutanese paper for jackets for one of Ripley's books that was in production at Smithsonian Press. During the expedition, Ripley periodically commented from far afield, noting delays, illnesses, shortages of equipment, and even the lack of sweet chutney of the kind that is commonplace in New Delhi. The record shows how Ripley kept his eyes on the big picture as well as the details. For want of local aircraft, Ripley, at the end of the trip, flattened once again by a severe case of dysentery, had to call in medevac assistance from India's air force and later sent profuse thanks to the officer who had arranged to save him.

To be sure, the Ripleys enjoyed hobnobbing with royalty

every bit as much as they tolerated being cold and soaking wet in the wild, as long as finding new or interesting birds was in prospect. Palaces, cathedrals, and museums were also there to be explored. In his treasured Asia, Ripley often managed to study nature in the good company of various noblemen and other well-heeled dignitaries. He visited the Maharaja of Jaipur's marble palace, eating pâté sandwiches while watching a tiger at a kill. He called on the jewel-encrusted King of Nepal. A host in Calcutta was Sir David Ezra, "a nabob of the old style," who lived in an enormous house and made his way around town aboard wheezing, chauffeured Rolls-Royces of 1920s vintages. From Sir David, member of a Jewish family that had moved to India from Baghdad and made fortunes in real estate and trade, Ripley received as a gift the well-preserved skin of a beautiful, extinct pink-headed duck, which he described as a "strangely colored long-necked bird, mostly chocolate brown with a bright Schiaparelli 'shocking' tone of pink on the neck and head." The skin was "a poor treasure indeed, compared to the living bird," said Ripley, "but what a fantastic specimen."[11]

Nepal at Last

Few places captivated Ripley as much as what was called the "Indian Region" encompassing India's northern provinces and beautiful Nepal and its lofty Himalayas. Nepal was controlled by Hindu maharajas with little interest in Western religions or culture, and up to the 1940s, few foreigners had been allowed to travel within the country beyond the Kathmandu Valley, site of the government seat. Knowledge of the region's birds was scant, wrote Ripley in his 1953 book, *Search for the Spiny Babbler*, consisting largely of studies compiled by a resident British naturalist named Brian Hodgson, who had lived there from 1821 to 1843. Hodgson's work on birds was "monumental," said Ripley, including the documentation of 563 species that hunters brought in to him from outlying areas. Fully 150 of these were new to science, and studying them with care a century later became "a most fertile field." Overall, said Ripley,

> the last forty years had seen a tremendous growth in evolutionary studies with the development of genetics. Parallel with this had come a great interest in studies of the evolution of species in nature. The initial steps in evolution, the isolation of continuous populations, the creation of geographical subspecies, recognizable subgroups within a species, had become a most fertile field of evolutionary research. The long continuous chain of the Himalayas with its profusion of species would be a veritable gold mine for such research.[12]

Many of Hodgson's specimens, stored at the British Museum, had become "worn and discolored" and, said Ripley, new material was desperately needed. After World War II, having managed despite the warfare to become generally familiar with the fauna of the Indian Region, he became eager to "range into the back country, in western and eastern Nepal where no collectors had ever been, and to try to make a thorough sampling of the avifauna."[13] One species of special interest was a mountain quail not seen by scientists since the 1880s. Another favorite was the spiny babbler, of which only five examples from Hodgson's times survived in tatters at the British Museum, and none had been recorded from the wild since Hodgson's times.

During the winter of 1946–47, Ripley and his assistant, Edward Migdalski, and the usual array of porters and taxidermists were in the Indian Region collecting birds for Yale and the Smithsonian. During their initial efforts to gain entry to Nepal in 1947, reported the historian Michael Lewis, Ripley had given Nepalese officials the impression that he was close to India's prime minister, Jawaharlal Nehru, and that Nehru was personally interested in his work. Word got around, infuriating both Nehru and Ali and raising suspicions of neo-imperialism among sensitive Indian leaders. Rumors had been circulating that internationally funded bird studies were cover-ups for research on the use of migrating birds as carriers of disease. In a strongly stated letter, Ali chided Ripley for "exploiting the supposed great friendship with Nehru in order to get admission into interior Nepal" and urged him to "make a bee-line" for New Delhi to mend the fences.[14] Ripley and Ali worked hard to ward off the germ warfare accusations and discontinued their use of US government funding for their bird studies. The flap blew over in the mid-1970s, clearing Ali's good name, but not without his accusing Ripley of having been indiscreet by telling the *New Yorker* writer Geoffrey T. Hellman too much in his 1950 profile. The dogs had barked in the night, said Ali, and the caravan had moved on. But the yelping carried on for two decades.

In New Delhi that 1946–47 winter, at a luncheon organized by George Merrell, the US chargé d'affaires, Ripley explained his interest in the birds of Nepal to Colonel Rana, a Nepalese official. Emphasizing that he was neither an economic royalist nor a missionary, he won a commitment from the colonel to approach the maharajah-prime minister, second in rank next to the king, and request permission to travel the unknown hinterlands. Eventually there came back a disappointing telegram, citing logistical issues, that offered Ripley's party a limited opportunity to conduct field research, not in remote western and eastern regions, but only within fifteen miles of Kathmandu, the capital. Ripley enthusiastically accepted, spent a month collecting birds within the mandated radius, and prepared a proposal "outlining the vital need for a ornithological exploration of outer Nepal, trying if possible to infuse some of my sense of excitement in the cause . . . which had been sharpened by the work that we were already doing." He and Ali were gambling that eventually they would be allowed to leave the arid plains where Buddha was born and get the access they sought, to "climb up into the river valleys, into the unknown mountains."[15] At the scruffy border town of Raxaul, hot, dirty, and tired, they boarded a small train for the rough four-hour, thirty-mile ride through increasingly beautiful scenery to Kathmandu.

Once in Kathmandu's valley, Ripley and his team began collecting such birds as they could find. Soon after arrival, they were summoned to an audience with the maharaja and responded to questions from his staff about the nature and purpose of the expedition. Stiff at the outset, the meeting warmed when Ripley entertained the court's military leaders by describing the team's layover in crowded Paris en route from the United States to India, which involved running out of cash and, with all hotels fully booked, having to spend a night at a *maison de bon accueil* (brothel).

Court ceremonies to which Ripley was invited featured glimpses of Nepal's king, flanked by high priests dressed in orange-colored gold brocade and sporting an elaborate crown studded with diamonds and emeralds, and progress toward discussing the travel specifics with him. The requested travel permits were granted without delay. "I only wished that I had more time and funds, for His Highness seemed keen to let us go as far as we wished," wrote Ripley, who made haste to pack up, attend a farewell audience with the king, and move his team northward toward the mountains.[16]

For three months ending in February 1949, Ripley's team ventured far beyond Kathmandu to spend six weeks in the Karnali River region of western Nepal, followed by a "similar period" along the Kosi River region at the foot of snow-plumed Mount Everest. As many as sixty-seven "coolies," as Ripley called these porters, were recruited to carry food and equipment for the expedition, some of them riding on bullock carts or elephants' necks but most relying on their own bare feet even at high, snowy altitudes along primitive mountain trails. Feeding this small army became a frequent challenge, as did finishing breakfast and decamping in time to find birds at the early-morning peak of their activity. Many were the mornings that found a frustrated Ripley bustling around the campsite trying to hurry things up but receiving the dreaded refrain from a local official: "Coolies taking food, sir, but just now coming."[17]

The team failed to rediscover the mountain quail, but its accomplishments were considerable. He had, said Ripley, sighted ten bird species not previously recorded in Nepal. And he had described eight new subspecies from Nepal, birds "which differed from their neighbors in some obvious character of color or size." He was able to document the "startling disappearance of bird and animal life between one thousand and seven thousand feet in altitude, where farming and deforestation had worked such havoc," including a number of species that may have gone extinct.[18]

One morning, on a hillside in the far west of Nepal, he came upon a flock of unfamiliar birds flicking their tails. Most flew at the sound of the gun, but after a short search Ripley found his prize, a brown bird the size of an American robin or an English blackbird. Subsequent research confirmed it was the first spiny babbler collected in 106 years. The single specimen, Ripley said, "proved beyond a doubt that the species still existed."[19]

Writing his spiny babbler book several years later, Ripley filled its pages with cheerful accounts of trekking in cold weather, food shortages, tangles with Indian and Nepalese bureaucrats, restless nights in tiger country, and delays with foot-dragging coolies "just now coming." The frustrations and dangers notwithstanding, he ended the book with a sentimental passage affirming his passionate love for the country's wildlands and wildlife:

> I had that vision with me always—the great peaks, the purple hills below, the mountain villages with their laughter, their horns echoing faintly along the valleys. Then, too, the birds, flocks of them, calling to each other, flying free from ridge to ridge. I had seen all of this and it was distilled, preserved clearly for an instant of time, a microcosm in the high hills of Nepal.[20]

The Charms of Litchfield

During the 1950s, Ripley spent much of his time in Litchfield. He was a part-time country squire during the summers and on the weekends, enjoying rides on his favorite horse, named Patches, horse shows and other such events, house guests, relaxed Sunday lunches, teas, and of course the ducks. The pretty little town of Litchfield is nestled in the shadow of the Berkshires in northern Connecticut. Founded in 1720, it had a population of some five thousand by 1950 and a lively history as an economic and intellectual center. It attracted dairy farmers, small mills and light industries, and students at the nation's first law school (Aaron Burr was its first pupil). In the nineteenth century, flocks of New Yorkers and other summer people came to enjoy its forests, rivers, streams, lakes, and sandy beaches. Ripley family members have long been settled in houses scattered around a two-thousand-acre parcel of Litchfield land that Ripley's great grandfather Sidney Dillon acquired in 1877.

In Litchfield, Ripley somehow found time to participate in community affairs. For half a century he served on the board of the Litchfield Historical Society, working hard and successfully to curb one increment of sprawl: persuading the board not to abandon its historic building on the handsome Village Green for a less central location where a new structure could be built. He was also a board member of the White Memorial Foundation, private owner of a four-thousand-acre, well-forested nature park near town that is richly endowed with wildlife in a natural setting. There Ripley led a drive to preserve a habitat for wild turkeys, which to this day are thriving in the park. For many years starting in the late 1960s, he served as well on the board of the Forman School in Litchfield, which had been founded in 1930 by his sister Julie Forman and her husband, John Forman, to address the needs of boys and girls with learning disabilities. Though Ripley was not a regular attendee at the meetings of these boards, he could not stay away entirely. "I'm a rooted person," he told the *Washington Post*'s Phil Casey.[21]

He spent much of his Litchfield time in the company of his ducks. Often that flock suffered grievous losses from predators or bad weather. The catastrophic 1955 Hurricane Diane flooded the brook leading to the duck pond, causing damage "beyond comprehension." During one severe winter, Ripley crawled gingerly out on thin ice to rescue wood ducks that had literally been frozen in. He relocated a great horned owl that had killed and eaten one of the young wood ducks. Other predators against which Ripley waged war included mink, weasels, snapping turtles, and rats. Dogs chased two terrified geese to death. Duckling production was also inhibited by rot, by a fungus or mold that killed eggs, and by periodic flooding from severe storms that destroyed or severely damaged Ripley's carefully built ponds and waterways. Daily duckling deaths took place during hatching times. Ripley endured the setbacks stoically. Aviculturists, he noted, "have an amazing way of being able to bounce back and retain their enthusiasm in the face of losses and tragedies."[22]

In a short paper, Ripley offered advice about managing waterfowl on country estates, a widespread practice in places as distant as China and as close by as New York City, where he had heard of someone keeping ducks in a penthouse. The cries of fowls cheer and animate the human abode, he said, calling them "the music of the rustic regiment" as performed in the "unthinking reverie" of Indian summer at the Litchfield ponds:

> There is something very pleasant and comforting in the delicate wild notes of the ducks as I sit watching them on a bright October afternoon. The little twisted white birches by the side of the pond are still. No breeze moves through the branches of the scarlet maples whose leaves flutter occasion-

ally to carpet the reflecting water. Only the ducks are not still. The gorgeous male Wood Ducks turn and twist on the water, displaying their wares of gaudy plumage before the hesitant females. Redheads, bills tucked under wings, half-asleep, wheel drowsily on the water with eyes now open now closed in that strange alert way ducks have. Others of many kinds rest, some on the grass preening their feathers endlessly, or coasting along by the banks dipping and prying for an elusive grub. A whistle of wings, every head is cocked sideways, and in comes a gaily crested little teal to land with a spatter and splash. Then a moment of hesitation while the ducks nearest him consider what his reception shall be before returning to unfinished business.[23]

Ripley also made good use of Litchfield as a hideaway when facing unpleasant obligations or potshots in New Haven or Washington. "This is the place Ripley considers home," reported the *Washington Post* reporter Phil Casey in a 1969 profile, "no matter where he goes or how long he must be away. It's a side of him not visible amidst the pomp and ceremony which attends his life in Washington."[24] Litchfield was where he wrote, read, and thought. He was fun to go walking with, said Mary Ripley, and good at identifying birds by their voices.

In recent times the Ripley daughters have made frequent use of Litchfield for recreation and also as board members, advisers, and officers of what is now known as the Livingston Ripley Waterfowl Conservancy (LRWC), a nonprofit organization founded by Dillon and Mary Ripley. Dedicated to the management and breeding of endangered waterfowl species at home and abroad, LWRC takes credit for bringing a number of them back from the brink, with captive breeding programs and survival planning for rare species. One notable success has been the Hawaiian nene goose, once down to fifty individuals but currently back up to five hundred or more on the island of Maui. In 2015, the LWRC scored the first captive-breeding success for the long-tailed duck, an endangered seabird found along the US Atlantic coast. A visit to the LWRC property, adjacent to a family home on Duck Pond Road, is likely to include a briefing from an enthusiastic volunteer or staff member on the current status of breeding efforts and education activities.

Mr. Ripley Goes to Washington

In Washington in the early 1960s, pressure was quietly building to carry Ripley and his family off in an unexpected direction. At the sprawling Smithsonian Institution, the vast national storehouse that dominates the Mall between the Capitol and the Washington Monument, the search for a new secretary (director) to replace the retiring Leonard Carmichael was getting under way. On the search committee formed in 1963 to propose a new secretary to the Institution's public-private Board of Regents—only the eighth since the Smithsonian was founded in 1846—were several people already well known to Ripley. One was Crawford Greenewalt, a corporate CEO who was also an expert on hummingbirds and photographing them. Another was John Nicholas Brown, of the powerhouse family that had been dominant in Rhode Island business and cultural circles since the seventeenth century. A third was the entomologist and Washington insider Caryl P. Haskins. It was Greenewalt who took the lead in approaching Ripley, visiting his lab at the Peabody to interview him and eventually offering him the job.

The committee found him at a moment of transition in his Yale circumstances. Whitney Griswold had died. Ripley felt uncomfortable with his successor as Yale's president, King-

man Brewster, who offered him few assurances about his future there. Ripley was outgrowing the old Peabody. "My roots
were shaken," he said. So here he was, at age forty-nine, with
an energetic wife and three daughters, aged seven to twelve,
in Yale's "homey" atmosphere but no clear sense of what the
future held for him. At the same time, he said, "I was very
familiar with the Smithsonian and did have quite strong opinions about what it was like then and what I could visualize its
possibly evolving into." Ripley found it a "dusty" place with
an "Edwardian if not Victorian demeanor, a tiny budget," and
"very parochial." But, just as the Peabody had been, it was
also a "sleeping beauty." In May 1963, after an intensive bout
of soul searching and listing pros and cons on yellow pads
during early-morning duck walks, overwhelming some family
misgivings, Mr. Ripley resolved to go to Washington. "We
all wanted to stay with what we knew," said Ripley's middle
daughter, Rosemary. "But our mother said that life is like a
book; you close one chapter and open another. Now we're closing the New Haven chapter."[25]

No one took the news harder than Ripley's mentor and
close friend, the Yale ecologist Evelyn Hutchinson, who called
it personally an "awful blow." "I suppose it is the most responsible job of its kind in the world as all the museums and galleries as well as the zoo in Washington are under the aegis of
the Smithsonian and its secretary," he wrote. "I think he is the
perfect man, having a good feeling for art and archaeology as
well as natural history, and all the right connections . . . there
is a very real problem generated by the approaching extinction
of the learned man of wealth who has professional standards,
public spirit, and amateur enthusiasms."[26] No one filled that
bill more precisely than Dillon Ripley.

CHAPTER FIVE

Defining a New Culture

Upon arriving in Washington in 1964, Ripley surprised even close friends with his drive and impatience while launching new Smithsonian initiatives. In several ways he tried to awaken the Smithsonian by paying more attention to popular movements and styles and their roots. During the later years of the turbulent 1960s, Ripley also opened wide the Smithsonian's doors and tried hard to make the broad public —including angry demonstrators marching on Washington— feel welcome inside. Ripley was at the top of his form during those busy years, as he pursued dreams of cultural excellence and advancement in social justice, with the Smithsonian exercising national leadership.

Building a livelier Smithsonian was not an easy matter in the Washington of those times. Despite the polish the stylish Kennedys had applied from the White House, it was widely felt in the 1960s that the town remained culturally, socially, and intellectually a provincial place. Washington's elite seemed largely content with a city that did not offer the widespread cultural amenities—or audiences—of a New York, Chicago, or San Francisco. "You can lead a middle class burgher to the *Mona Lisa*," wrote the *New York Times* columnist Russell Baker, a Washington fixture for many years. "But you

can't make him surrender his martini hour for Couperin."[1]
Between Memorial Day and Labor Day, for want of good air-
conditioning, the drowsy capital got even sleepier as vacation-
ing leaders fled to the mountains and the seashore.

Congress and the Smithsonian's governing regents often
resisted change. Trying to make modest advances, let alone
launch big new ideas, Ripley had to deal with staff people such
as the career administrator who was known as "The Abomi-
nable No-Man," as Ripley stated in his valedictory 1984 annual report, "for his unwavering diligence in barring the door
against innovation." The goals Ripley set included the democratic one of alerting the public to its ownership of something
far grander than "a dusty vitrine containing insects impaled
on little pins, their names penned in a language as dead as the
halls' appeal," where workers "labored in Stygian gloom. Ripley found major gaps in the institution's curriculum, especially
in environmental science, and sensed that it was "incumbent
on America's preeminently national museum to take its place
as a leader both in this country and abroad."[2]

Along the Mall, to be sure, the Smithsonian's treasures were
on display, free of charge to visitors, every day but Christmas,
to the delight of millions. There was the Hope Diamond, the
Star-Spangled Banner, the beaver hat that President Lincoln
wore when he was shot, the First Ladies' dresses on manne-
quins, a Mighty Wurlitzer jukebox, a rare 1701 Stradivari cello,
dinosaurs, the artist James McNeill Whistler's famed Peacock
Room, the ventriloquist Charlie McCarthy in full regalia, glis-
tening 1920s Packard cars. One cannot overstate the thrill of
experiencing these treasures and countless others in the Smithsonian's vast collections. Conserving and displaying those powerful objects were in themselves notable accomplishments.

Ripley's predecessor, the psychologist Leonard Carmichael, had achieved some progress during his decade in office. New wings had been added to what is now known as the National Museum of Natural History, and poorly designed and poorly lit exhibition halls had been improved. A new attraction on the Mall, the Museum of History and Technology (now the National Museum of American History), was nearing completion in 1964, when Carmichael stepped aside. Storage space had been found for vast and rapidly growing collections of catalogued objects. Useful scientific work had been done in the labs and out in the field. Improvements were being made at the National Zoo, a Smithsonian bureau, after decades of accumulated neglect. Visitors to the six Smithsonian museums had grown in number from 3,290,000 in 1953 to 10,309,000 in 1963.

But much badly needed transformational work remained undone. Sorting out the "nation's attic" required tact and skill. Consolidation was in order. Government-owned parking lots and unused buildings cried out to be put to better use. Most of the now familiar structures along Washington's iconic National Mall were yet to be built. Physically, its rows of bland government-issue buildings lacked luster, as did the furnishings within them. The Mall was mostly open space. Tiny budgets for cultural and educational activities and for research limited the scope of the science and art institutions that were in place. And above all, as Ripley saw it, the Smithsonian needed to open up.

Adding Sparkle and Substance

Ripley started close to home. Soon after arriving in 1964, he began to redecorate his office in the red-sandstone Smithsonian Castle on the Mall. He banished humdrum government-issue furnishings in favor of Victorian pieces dating from the many years in residence of the physicist Joseph Henry, the Institution's first secretary, and his family. In keeping with his long-standing belief that museums should be not storehouses but activists in close touch with their communities, Ripley uprooted the elegant statue of Henry that still adorns the entryway from the Mall. For many years, Henry had looked inward at the Castle doorways; Ripley reversed him so he could gaze outward at the busy pedestrian traffic along the Mall.

To engage children, he restored a 1920s carousel and in 1967 installed it on the Mall, right outside the Institution's headquarters, to the delight of young and old customers, who flocked to the site for rides aboard thirty-three assorted animals and two chariots. He applauded a kite-flying contest on the Mall, ran races featuring quarter horses from Oklahoma, sent the assistant secretary for science and research at the Smithsonian, David Challinor, off on a futile search for racing camels similar to those he had ridden as a child in Egypt. He wanted a Southern Railway locomotive not just to sit there, but to move whistling down the tracks. Inside the halls he wanted to see the Institution's museum's musical instruments used, not left hanging inside cases where in the winter they cracked as the wood expanded and "snuffled" in the summer as water dripped out of them.

In 1965, he founded a Smithsonian Associates group, modeled after the one that had helped bring Yale's Peabody Museum alive. In return for annual membership dues of as little as ten dollars, said an admiring *Washington Post*, the Associates group provided "culture-wary Washingtonians" with ample opportunities to "explore the arts, the sciences, and humanities." The Washington version soon buzzed with lectures, sem-

inars, craft workshops, behind-the-scenes tours, programs for
children whose parents were not allowed to accompany them,
field trips, discounts at an expanding array of museum shops,
and—most important of all—special parking privileges on
Smithsonian lots. Said the program administrator, Carolyn
Amundson: "The best thing about the Smithsonian Associates
is that it is constantly evolving. People keep coming up and ask-
ing what we are going to be doing next and we have to shrug.
. . . But it's more fun this way, more flexible." Within three
years the program had attracted some eight thousand members
in the Washington area, and Ripley was keen to take it national.[3]

In 1965, the Kennedy Center, which like the National Gallery of Art was technically a Smithsonian bureau even though
it had its own board of directors and bylaws, was taking shape
as a major new cultural force in Washington. As an ex officio
board member, Ripley had no voting power. He showed his
colors anyhow, proposing ways to counter his apprehension
that the grand new performing arts center was "being planned
for a snappy kind of people coming in mink coats." In a letter to the powerful impresario and former White House arts
adviser Roger Stevens, then the Center's chair, he advocated
lively and affordable programming for broad audiences to
avoid its becoming a "lifeless marble shell." If elitist Kennedy
Center programmers were doing no more than "creating a
more lavish setting for what already goes on in Washington,"
he wrote, a "great opportunity" would be neglected.[4]

Defining Culture More Broadly

As an example of a popular alternative to highbrow culture,
he said, he could cite the Smithsonian's own Folklife Festival
on the Mall, soon to become a prized fixture each July. The

festival was the brainchild of the operatic singer and theatrical producer James Morris, hired in 1966 to direct the Smithsonian's performing arts programs. Looking over the Institution from an outsider's standpoint, Morris found a senior management team composed of older all-white men, all "products of Eastern style and privilege." He pondered ways to expand their vision, using the Institution's priceless assets to bring to life a robust American popular culture lying outside the limits of what is conventionally perceived as cultural.

A Smithsonian folk festival, Morris concluded, "would enliven the collections and be a central focus of a re-invigorated National Mall that would become an open-air forum and classroom. A festival could also cross racial, class, and social boundaries." It would showcase what Ripley later called "real Americans doing real things with their hands — crafts that stem back to the roots of our culture."[5]

In early 1967, Morris went to Ripley with a proposal for a Smithsonian Festival of American Folklife. Ripley said OK, reducing the budget from the requested $8,900 to a paltry $4,900 for fees and transportation. Ripley was not convinced that much could happen with so little money, but charged Morris to "have us a festival, in which we had people shearing sheep, weaving wool, making dulcimers, throwing pots, cooking short ribs. And doing American folk-country things — dancing, music, eats, and so on, the sort of thing that people can do thoughtfully and creatively in a long hot summer." Recalling his childhood stay in Paris, when he could visit the Louvre and ride the Tuileries Gardens carousel as facets of a single experience, he wondered how he could get the Smithsonian "out on the grass, onto the Mall."[6]

In the light of the emerging national wave of interest in folk music that had slowly been building since the 1950s, Morris hit the pavement to seek additional support for this part of the Smithsonian festival. Artists such as Pete Seeger and Woody Guthrie had found enthusiastic audiences for songs with strong political content. Wrote Peter Yarrow of the popular Peter, Paul, and Mary group: "Singing the music of the people, particularly singing it together, was not merely a symbolic act. It was, literally, an act of liberation and an assertion of freedom."[7] Popular festivals celebrating this music attracted widening attention, including a 1962 *Time* magazine cover story on Joan Baez for which this author did the principal reporting. Though regarded by some as an inconsequential coffeehouse folksinger, Baez had established a strong foothold. So also had such other new faces as Bob Dylan (before his controversial conversion to the electric guitar), the Kingston Trio, and Peter, Paul, and Mary. Likewise gaining in stature were folk artists considered more authentic, such as the blind guitarist and singer Doc Watson, the legendary African American performer Huddie Ledbetter ("Lead Belly"), and the coal miner Dock Boggs. The songs these artists sang—"Tsena Tsena," "Goodnight Irene," "Midnight Special," "If I Had a Hammer" —had become part of a new national culture triggering debate, as Yarrow put it, about "the notion of culture itself."

Morris's search led him to the folklorist Ralph Rinzler, who had helped assemble a benchmark folk music festival in Newport, Rhode Island, and was well known to small bands of traditional musicians keeping their craft alive in the nation's backwoods, as well as to more widely known figures. Morris brought Rinzler aboard as a consultant, and together they fashioned the Smithsonian's festival. Others suggested potters, weavers, storytellers, and other prospective participants.

Organizations as diverse as New Mexico's state police and a Louisiana fish-processing company helped out. Performers accepted $100 honoraria in return for the chance to display their talents at a national museum.

A remarkable 450,000 people turned out for the first festival, in 1967, which featured a wide variety of crafts and performances, from Indian music to polka music, basketmaking to silversmithing. The striking thing about it, a delighted Ripley thought, was

> the quiet and immense satisfaction of the people who came to watch and listen, sitting around and taking it all in, while their children romped nearby on the grass. It was a moving spectacle and one that underscored the principle that a museum, to be a museum in the best sense of the word, must live and breathe both within and without.[8]

"One night in one of those early festivals," he recalled, "Mary and I joined a group of tribal people from the Mohawk nation, and danced under the full moon in the middle of the Mall, just us and nobody else, to a drum, and we absolutely loved it. We felt transported into another world, and they were very sweet about it."[9] In its early years, the festival focused tightly on American folklore traditions, from basketweaving to local interpretations of Irish dance. Ripley proved far-sighted in predicting that the festival would become an annual Washington event by popular demand.

Starting in 1974, with the inclusion of presentations from the African diaspora, the festival went global under Rinzler's gifted direction. Ripley took pride in the shift, applauding the Smithsonian's championing of the idea that the festival's events should enlarge America's ability to get past feeling that ethnic origins are not quite part of the American dream.

Building folk art into the program of the Renwick, a small decorative arts gallery that belongs to the Smithsonian, Ripley emphasized the point by celebrating diversity in some of its exhibitions. So did an idea that soon became a festival fixture: picking the traditional culture of a single US state and, mindful of where that art originated, emphasizing its geographical origins as well, showing how "dashing and beautifully turned-out" immigrant versions at times outshone the originals. So, while the festival has presented musical offerings from all over the tuneful Americas, in 2006 it also proudly featured the songs and dances of Latino Chicago.

The Folklife Festival survived even a bitter fight between Rinzler and Morris, whose programs often ran in the red and who made many enemies. Rinzler made efforts to elbow Morris aside and deal directly with Ripley, and chided Morris for paying insufficient attention to the festival. "The history of bogus charges, non-existent memoranda, and demands for autonomy had created a toxic environment that corrupted healthy deliberations," Morris retorted. "When discussions began to trade in hyperbole rather than rhetoric, I was appalled. When hyperbole became virulent, I resigned as festival producer."[10] But the festival itself carried on somehow, achieving star status for its twelve-week run the US Bicentennial summer of 1976, with an audience of 5 million and a $6 million budget. For the duration it remained an annual hit, scoring yet another victory for Ripley and popular culture. In introducing the seventh festival he wrote:

It seems fitting to explain again why a museum such as the Smithsonian Institution is concerned with living performers. We are a conservation organization, and it seems to us that conservation extends to human cultural practices. The possibility of using a museum which is essentially a historical documentary museum as a theater of live performance where people actually show that the objects in cases were made by human hands, and are still being made, practiced on, worked with, is a very valuable asset for our role as a preserver and conservator of living forms and it should be understood in those terms.[11]

To rebut contrary accusations, Ripley went on the offensive by arguing that "it is not a kind of razzle-dazzle, a vaudeville show that we put on. It is rather a demonstration of the vitality of those cultural roots which surround us and are so often overlooked. The fact that we celebrate ethnic diversity in our culture is, I think, extremely important . . . it is worthwhile being proud, not fiercely proud, but gently and happily proud, of the continuance of these cultural roots and their observances and practices that we celebrate." Fieldworkers assembling the various components of the festival strove mightily to make it "exciting and alive," wrote the museum historian William S. Walker in his book *A Living Exhibition*, but also to have it reach beyond entertainment to become an authentic experience free from the taint of commercialism and the participation of "folk-pop performers."[12]

Smithsonian scouts would delve deeply into rural areas to screen out revivalists and polished professional folk performers in favor of amateurs who had learned their skills from within their families or communities. At times their selection criteria became so rigid that some practitioners who were not included complained vigorously, as in the instance of Italian American musicians wanting to perform contemporary music rather than the older tunes more highly prized by sometimes overzealous Smithsonian researchers. A Maryland saddlemaker, said Walker, was excluded because he had received formal training as an apprentice and did not come from the western United States, where master craftspeople in this field were expected to be found.

Regardless of such outbreaks of rough spots, both among disgruntled staff members and among performers and craftspeople, the popular Folklife Festival evolved into a mature force showing the potential of what Ripley called "open education." He saw museums as places where visitors would receive instruction not in formal classroom settings but by the encouragement of "independent exploration" and "freedom of movement both inside and outside museum spaces." The informal style of the festival, enabling free exchanges between practitioners and audiences under tents or in open spaces, would mark a counterpoint to the more formal styles of professors or volunteer docents working within closed museum gallery spaces, supplementing educational activities on the preschool level all the way to the postdoctoral level. This emphasis on open teaching in open spaces, radical in a community where auditorium lectures had long prevailed, has since become commonplace among museum educators.[13]

New York City's staid American Museum of Natural History launched a popular street fair called West Side Day. "Who are all these people?" asked the museum's conservative 1970s board chair as he warily eyed throngs of absorbed visitors to the event. The move toward openness and dialogue indoors, as well as out on the street, thrives today. At Yale, the art historian John Walsh builds an entire ambulatory course for graduate students around the careful study of a small number of individual paintings, each considered separately and reviewed during group discussions rather than by means of questions and answers. Digital technologies enable Walsh's messages to extend far afield.

As the museum educators Rika Burnham and Elliott Kai-Kee put it, there is a "growing consensus among museum educators in support of learner-centered approaches that emphasize students' active participation through discussion, with a corresponding de-emphasis for teachers on lecturing and other methods of imparting information."[14] Once again, in a field far away from his own intellectual roots, perhaps guided by his early experiences at a Montessori school and on the rich cultural playgrounds of his beloved Paris, Dillon Ripley led the way. He saw open education at museums as an integral part of Lyndon Johnson's Great Society. He foresaw a leading role for museums in bringing about no less than a cultural revolution, transforming American society.

As Walker explains in his book, there was intellectually a sharp division in the emerging field of museum education. The media analyst Marshall McLuhan joined Ripley in championing free-choice learning — a means of empowering museum visitors and making them less passive by placing them in relatively unstructured situations where they could learn on their own. The cultural historian Jacques Barzun, continued Walker, "believed that overwhelming people with an array of objects and then suggesting that they sort it out for themselves was a recipe not for empowerment but for apathy and confusion." Ripley found flaws in the exhibits at the Smithsonian's new Museum of History and Technology, which he considered lacking in diversity and in respect for contemporary culture. He saw the success of the Folklife Festival as a validation of his less traditional approaches. He made it into what Walker called the "rebellious stepchild" in the Smithsonian galaxy, with some officials viewing it as an "out of control experiment in need of reform" and others seeing it as a "vital asset" burnishing the Institution's reputation.[15]

Launching a Neighborhood Museum

Each summer the Folklife Festival draws strong and enthusiastic multiracial crowds despite frequently hot or rainy weather. Notwithstanding its success, Ripley and his close associate, the assistant secretary of the Smithsonian, Charles Blitzer, still worried about the composition of the Smithsonian's audiences. They remained concerned that its "marble palaces" on the Mall attracted "so few people who might be described as being from the depressed classes, people who were often black, underfed intellectually, and seemed to have the most urgent need for cultural media in which to associate and learn something." Blitzer, a New York–born political scientist with ample credentials as a champion of liberal humanism, was the deputy Ripley leaned on hardest when trouble or opportunity arose. Ripley called him "my confidential confidant to give me advice and do a lot of the bulldogging." Blitzer cared a lot about cultural communications, global and local. After his years with Ripley he spent another decade as director of the Woodrow Wilson International Center for Scholars, another Ripley offspring.

The concern that Ripley and Blitzer shared about museums and communities crystallized, after many conversations, into Ripley's belief that "we ought to have a museum for underprivileged people in a run-down neighborhood." Ripley broached the idea at an "extremely boring" conference in 1966 in opulent Aspen, Colorado, where experts, including several from the Smithsonian, had gathered for three days to discuss the future of museums. "The only significant thing that happened at that meeting," recalled Ripley, "was that one of us said, 'We, at the Smithsonian, have been kicking around the idea that we'd like to start a museum in a very poor, rather disadvantaged section of a major city for the people who live there . . . take your museum, somehow, out, have it there, and have it participated in, by the local people.'"[16]

There ensued what he described as a "deadly pause" at the thought of placing treasured masterpieces in such a venue. "We could *never* do *that*," said one curator. "It would mean exposing our masterpieces to these hands to be sullied by them," confirming Ripley's impression that such people "feel that the art is really for them and their peers, at higher levels of appreciation."[17] They came away from the conference "quite depressed" and ever more determined to give the idea a try. Ripley sponsored a search not for a drug-ridden ghetto area with a lot of street traffic and violence, but a more settled, traditionally black neighborhood few of whose residents would ever venture into the downtown Smithsonian's "mausoleums."

With help from the psychologist Caryl Marsh, a Smithsonian consultant who was well known in Washington neighborhoods, Ripley's team studied and rejected several parts of the city before the search narrowed to Anacostia, a predominantly black section of Washington across the river from the Capitol. The neighborhood's history can be traced back to Captain John Smith, who visited there in 1608, but the community had been reduced to a pocket of deep poverty in recent years. Many black households containing eight or nine children had incomes of $4,000 a year. There the Smithsonian team found the abandoned Carver movie theater, spruced it up, and established the Anacostia Neighborhood Museum. It maintained links to the Mall institutions but also a high degree of autonomy with a young, community-based director, John Kinard, a Howard University graduate, self-ordained minister, and Peace Corps alumnus with a background in community organization and civil rights leadership. This leader, whom Ripley found to be "vigorous and decisive," received much input from a community advisory council. Ripley recalled in his book *The Sacred Grove* that this team engaged in "long and prayerful" planning meetings at a church rather than the more tightly structured conference room discussions to which the Smithsonian staff was accustomed.[18]

Skepticism was rampant, with widespread doubt that the Smithsonian could cross the river and effectively meet the needs of a poor black community. Tensions bubbled over from time to time, as when, said Caryl Marsh in a lengthy *Museum News* article, "the white middle class volunteer lady is no longer welcome to do a job that a black person might be hired to do."[19] As Ripley recalled, "We would go in, and we quickly trained ourselves to say nothing unless we were asked to make a comment." But relations warmed when the community started requesting advice, and a friendly spirit came to prevail. Planning meetings were well attended.

There were no guards at the museum when it opened on September 15, 1967, with an eighty-four-piece band on hand and Ripley posing beside a plastic dinosaur named Uncle Beazley, and there was no vandalism either. This was a "truly important event in the history of museums," Ripley said. Four thousand people attended. Early exhibits varied widely, from a mockup of a Mercury space capsule that children could touch to a replica of an 1890 country store and a small zoo. Later, popular objects of attention shifted away from miniature efforts to replicate the vast Smithsonian and concentrated on matters of more immediate concern to residents of an urban African American community and its history. Kinard did not flinch from covering disagreeable subjects such as rats and prison life.

The overall results have been mixed. The concept of "taking your museums to the people," as Ripley had advised his Aspen audience, has hardly swept the nation. Not every small neighborhood institution enjoys the kind of support from big national foundations that came to Anacostia with Ripley and his quiet advocates. Smithsonian staff members complain about technical matters. Some call the experiment a failure, with weak roots in the community and no well-defined mission, all but invisible in busy Washington. But with almost fifty years of its own history, the museum has survived periodic changes in name, mission statement, program emphasis, and a move to larger quarters. What is now called the Anacostia Community Museum has a current budget of several million dollars and a variety of activities. It has become a nationally recognized institution and a fixture and a "drop-in place for dropouts," according to one observer. "It has survived," said Ripley, "and that's important in itself."

The museum historian William Walker wrote that Ripley "was not alone in this endeavor of course, as a small number of leaders in the museum field began working on the project of connecting urban communities and museums. . . . The Anacostia Museum was the flagship project in the effort and a harbinger of things to come. . . . Remarkably, for a large, public institution, the Smithsonian was able to advance a pioneering, experimental project that challenged the staid foundations of American museums."[20]

Once when Ripley visited, he started a conversation with "a giant of a man in a rough jacket," a truck driver, who said he had been "scared" to visit the museums on the Mall. But his experience with the Anacostia had persuaded him to give it a try. "Yes, sir, you're getting me cultured before I know it." That statement was what Ripley had come to hear.[21]

Welcoming the Demonstrators

Ripley in the late 1960s also found himself immersed in social policy. Washingtonians who lived in the city's leafy northwest sections hardly ever visited the black ghettos of a city still as deeply segregated as Birmingham or Montgomery. They were indifferent to mounting demands for social justice that brought severe rioting to downtown Fourteenth Street after the assassination of Dr. Martin Luther King in 1968. Violence beset the Mall several times. One night a motorcycle policeman suffered a broken arm. Someone lost an eye to an ice pick. Beer bottles were thrown. Some feared vandalism, with pressures mounting to lock the doors along the Mall. Ripley took a different approach. He regarded the Mall buildings as "open havens" where demonstrators could rest, use the facilities, get away from tear gas and night sticks.

During the peace demonstration and march on November 15, 1969, reported *Smithsonian Year 1970*, the Museum of History and Technology hosted eighty-one thousand fugitives from bitterly cold weather and tear gas on Constitution Avenue. So many people jammed into the museum that some had to stand up all night. But the cafeteria opened up, it was warm, and, said Ripley, "everybody was very polite, there were no incidents. It was a great demonstration." Thank-you letters and phone calls came in from all over the country. During the May 1970 March on Washington, with rain pelting down and the Mall a quagmire, Smithsonian performers managed to stage an impromptu concert for drenched militants. "It was a source of some amazement that we condescended to get into the fray," Ripley recalled. "But it was very successful."[22]

On one celebrated occasion, Ripley sat down with a group of demonstrating museum workers whom the museum guards, decked out in full riot gear, were treating as if they were rioters and therefore "dangerous." "Some of them came forward," Ripley recalled. "Now take me out. How are you going to take me out? They were gentle indeed and lifted me up, as if I was a precious object, and conducted me out. Then I came back, and we all started laughing and joking and smiling." Even when things were touch and go at various times, Ripley said, "I wanted to make people feel that this was our constituency and our constituency was the nation."[23]

Baby Ripley and his mother. Photo: Courtesy of the Ripley family.

The coddled young Mr. Ripley.
Photo: Smithsonian Institution Archives

Dillon Ripley (age 3) and his much older siblings, New York City, winter 1916. From *left*: Constance Dillon Ripley, Dillon Ripley, Julia Rose Ripley, Louis Rose Ripley. Photo: Smithsonian Institution Archives

Ripley riding on his father's shoulders.
Photo: Smithsonian Institution Archives

Nepal Expedition, National Geographic Society/Smithsonian Institution/Yale University expedition, 1948, the quest for the rare mountain quail. Ripley asks residents in the village of Rekcha if they had spotted this elusive bird. None had. Photo: Smithsonian Institution Archives

Nepal research team group portrait, 1949, with prematurely balding Ripley at *center.* Photo: Smithsonian Institution Archives

Dillon Ripley and Mary Livingston Ripley aboard an Asian elephant.
Photo: Smithsonian Institution Archives

Above: Ripley studies bird specimens at his ornithology lab at Yale University's Peabody Museum, 1948. Photo: Smithsonian Institution Archives

Right: The Ripleys surround Indian ornithologist Sálim Ali during one of their innumerable research expeditions to India's hinterlands. Photo: Smithsonian Institution Archives

Left: The Ripleys at work in the backlands of India. Photo: Jehangir Gazdar/Woodfin Camp

Below: Far afield in Bhutan, 1968. Photo: Mary Livingston Ripley

Above: The Ripleys greet
President and Mrs. Lyn-
don B. Johnson. The President was convinced that
culture formed an integral
part of his Great Society,
and Smithsonian Secretary
Dillon Ripley took fruitful
advantage of this convic-
tion. Photo: Smithsonian
Institution Archives

Right: Ripley and President Lyndon Johnson: a
well-matched pair. Photo:
Smithsonian Institution

Ripley and a model of the university-like Smithsonian campus that he sought to build. Photo: Richard Howard

Above: Ripley welcomes
Britain's Queen Elizabeth
II at the Smithsonian
Castle in 1976. Facing
the Queen is then Vice
President Nelson Rocke-
feller. Photo: Smithsonian
Institution

Right: Ripley passes the
statue of the Smithso-
nian's first secretary,
Joseph Henry, as he
departs the Smithsonian
Castle. Ripley made a
striking point when he
asked that the statue be
turned so that Henry
would look outward at the
public on the Mall, not
inward at the building's
gloomy entryway. Photo:
Smithsonian Institution

Left: The dashing Secretary cuts the rug at a Renwick Gallery event. Photo: Smithsonian Institution

Below: Ever the showman, Ripley greets Sesame Street's Big Bird. Photo: Smithsonian Institution

Above: Ripley and his mascot, a fiberglass dinosaur named Uncle Beazley, at the grand opening of the Anacostia Neighborhood Museum. Photo: Smithsonian Institution

Right: Ripley aboard the carousel he brought to the Mall. Photo: Smithsonian Institution

Ripley at a 101st birthday event for fifth Secretary Charles
Greeley Abbott, along with two other former Secretaries:
Frank Alexander Wetmore and Leonard Carmichael.
Photo: Smithsonian Institution

Above: Top-hatted Ripley and Chief Justice Warren Burger, head of the Smithsonian's Board of Regents, ride President Ulysses Grant's carriage to the U.S. Bicentennial celebration. Photo: Smithsonian Institution

Right: Secretary Ripley in full regalia. Photo: Smithsonian Institution Archives

Secretary Ripley and waterfowl at his bird sanctuary in Litchfield,
Connecticut. Photo: Smithsonian Institution Archives

The newly retired Ripley cuddles ducklings in Litchfield.
Photo: Richard Howard

CHAPTER SIX

Displaying the Nation's Art

Ripley loved art. He took courses, wrote papers, often visited museums and historic sites. From the moment of his arrival at the Smithsonian, he signaled his resolve to ensure that it earned national and international prominence as an arts institution, even if some stepping on toes might be required.

Support for this aspiration could be found in the 1846 congressional legislation founding the Institution, which called for the transfer to its possession of all federally owned works of art as well as of natural history. The "programme of organization" put forth in 1847 by Joseph Henry, the Smithsonian's first secretary, called for the provision of space to display artworks and encourage those working in the field.[1] Justification could thus be found for the first Smithsonian building to contain a gallery of art even though, as Ripley conceded, the Institution would remain concentrated primarily on the sciences.

Most secretaries after Henry allowed the Smithsonian art collections to gather dust in obscure locations. A fire in 1865 destroyed all but a few pieces. Nonetheless, reported Paul Oehser in his book *The Smithsonian Institution*, its enthusiasm for art was later "slowly but surely rekindled" on the basis of contributions from well-off donors."[2] So in the historical record there was a clear if underused mandate for yet another bold Ripley initiative: to assemble and curate a significant national art collection.

In Lyndon and Lady Bird Johnson, riding high in Washington in the mid-1960s, Ripley found partners who maintained what he called an "implicit sense of reverence" for cultural leadership at the top end. They would do much to help the Institution become a prime element in the emerging Great Society and achieve fast-rising prestige as a national and international cultural capital. Both of Johnson's parents had been schoolteachers before they entered state politics in Texas. The president himself, as a young man working his way through college, had done some time in the classroom as well. He taught barely literate, dirt-poor Mexican and black fifth to eighth graders in the small Texas town of Cotulla and, wrote Charles Peters in his biography of Johnson, remained "determined to inspire a sense of hope in the beaten-down children" in his class.[3]

Johnson wanted people to shed the "stereotype notions that the public at large might have about him," Ripley said in his oral history for the LBJ Presidential Library. "Coming up from humble origins in Texas with perhaps a certain sense of feeling that people on the eastern side of the subcontinent of the United States were more aware of culture than people in Texas were, he too would love to have the feeling that his own administration had had a strong impact on the cultural life of Washington."[4]

Wrote a *Washington Post* critic, Philip Kennicott, in a 2014 piece celebrating the fiftieth anniversary of the Great Society: "In the extraordinarily active 89th Congress, which began in 1965, Johnson did something unprecedented in American history. He put art, culture, and beauty on the same footing as roads, rights, commerce, and security. If you want to understand Johnson's cultural agenda, you have to see it not as an appendage but integrally related to the War on Poverty and the Civil Rights Act of 1964."[5]

Little Man, Big Art

Ripley, soon after his arrival on the Washington scene, was quick to detect a cultural gap that offered an enormous opportunity for the Smithsonian and for Johnson: no museum in the capital had a top-quality modern art collection. Thanks to the gracious and discerning Mellon family, the National Gallery of Art could claim first-class holdings of European and American paintings and sculpture, but these works dated only up to about 1905. As a matter of policy in those times, the National Gallery refrained from collecting works by living or recently deceased artists. During his frequent travels, the keen-eyed Duncan Phillips had assembled a formidable if small collection for his family museum near Dupont Circle. But, said the *Washington Post* art critic Andrew Hudson, Phillips had bought art more to satisfy personal tastes than to build a scholarly survey of the field in a systematic way. The Corcoran Gallery of Art could claim solid American holdings but not the counterpart European examples that would provide perspective. In short, said Hudson, it would take a heavy infusion of contemporary paintings and sculpture to place Washington in a competitive position vis-à-vis the art world's major capitals. Something new and big was needed.

Accordingly, Ripley launched a discreet search for "*the* person who would have the seminal collection of modern art

nonpareil." He got a tip from Charles Cunningham, director of the Art Institute of Chicago, who casually mentioned
that a rags-to-riches Latvian immigrant and uranium investor
named Joseph Hirshhorn had a large collection and perhaps
could be persuaded to donate something to the Smithsonian's
National Collection of Fine Arts. Few knew exactly what this
trove consisted of in total, but reports had it that Hirshhorn
had amassed some ten thousand pieces: fifteen hundred sculptures, including pieces by Rodin, Maillol, Matisse, Calder,
and Picasso, as well as about forty-eight hundred paintings
and works on paper by equally illustrious US and European
artists. The flamboyant collector, five feet four in height and
given to unusual clothing such as an ankle-length mink coat,
was renowned for his cunning. Though never indicted for any
reason, he was thought at times to operate at the edges of the
law. He kept much of his collection out of public view at his
estate in rural Greenwich, Connecticut.

He did not buy art to make money, he said. As described
by Aline Saarinen in her 1958 book, *The Proud Possessors*, he
"became an art collector for two fundamental reasons. He
grew out of his early environment with a huge, often indis-
criminate but passionately real love for art." In addition, he
felt an "almost compulsive concern for the artist's welfare."[6]
Flush from having bailed out of the stock market just weeks
before the 1929 crash, he began to visit galleries in New York
and elsewhere on his own, following his impulses rather than
relying on professional advisers, as did the Rockefellers and
other prominent collectors.

His habit was not to buy single works on these expeditions,
but rather to make bulk purchases. Wrote Saarinen, "He
could no more think of buying a single object out of an ex-

hibition than he could dream of purchasing a single unit of a stock issue."[7] The result was a large if uneven collection. It was disparaged by some critics and by a few distinguished museum professionals, including Sherman Lee—an Asian and Early American art expert and the much admired director of the Cleveland Museum of Art. But most experts, including the influential *Washington Post* art critic Paul Richard, argued that the collection was of sufficient quality to justify the widespread interest in finding a permanent public home for it.

Wooing and landing Hirshhorn, a remarkable joint venture on the part of the Smithsonian Castle and the White House, reveals Ripley at the top of his game, moving the project along with incisive indirection. Initially, so as not to spook his target, he proposed only that Hirshhorn consider lending a work or two for temporary exhibition in Washington. Later, after reading the Saarinen book's Hirshhorn chapter, Ripley began to think more boldly. He and Smithsonian colleagues met with Abram Lerner, Hirshhorn's curator, who himself was not sure of the collection's total magnitude or value. Wanting to meet Hirshhorn, Ripley asked for help from his friend Roger Stevens, the well-connected Broadway producer and real estate mogul. Stevens contacted Hirshhorn's Greenwich neighbor, the redoubtable social doyenne Permelia Reed, who knew and liked Hirshhorn. She asked Stevens and Ripley to tea and, Ripley recalled, "she said right away, 'Of course, I'll do whatever I can to bring this together. Let's go and meet Joe.' She picked up the phone and rang him up. Soon after they went over to his house and met him." Ripley admired the "most beautiful sculptured landscaping and a wonderful driveway of Belgian cobbles, a lovely place and marvelous for his outdoor sculpture," including pieces by Rodin and a Giacometti dog.[8]

At that meeting, Ripley broached the idea of Hirshhorn handing over his entire collection as a gift to the United States and housing it in a federally funded Joseph A. Hirshhorn Museum and Sculpture Garden to be built on the Mall. At first, Ripley found, Hirshhorn was cool to the idea, or at least was putting up a front. But for all the uncertainties involved, he mellowed, and there began what Ripley called a firm friendship. Said Ripley: "Hirshhorn was so real. I love to talk turkey with people if they want to talk turkey."[9]

On May 21, 1965, Mrs. Johnson held a White House luncheon for the Hirshhorns. The guest list included high-ranking White House officials, Ripley, and Stevens, who played what Ripley called an "absolutely fundamental part" in the negotiations. The president stopped by briefly, but his appearance was crucial. "I must say it was an enormous success because the Hirshhorns were captivated by President and Mrs. Johnson," Ripley said in his LBJ Presidential Library oral history interview. "It was love at first sight."[10] The former Supreme Court justice Abe Fortas and his wife helped as well, attending the luncheon and, continued Ripley, playing "their own impressive and quiet part in imparting to the Johnsons the sense that this would indeed be a historic moment in the administration of the President." It was, Ripley said, a "pushover" requiring no real effort beyond getting a moment alone with the president to explain the importance of such an acquisition.

In August 1965, Mrs. Johnson and her daughter Lynda visited Greenwich. Following up, Hirshhorn wrote the president a warm letter dated September 21, 1965, stating that "Mrs. Johnson is darling and has completely charmed me." In the glow of these exchanges, with the White House aboard, Ripley began carefully working the Hirshhorn side to reel the project in. He orchestrated discussions about management under the Smithsonian umbrella, the size and placement on the Mall of the sculpture garden to showcase the most important Hirshhorn pieces, and the choice of an architect to design the museum building.

As word spread about the magnitude of Hirshhorn's holdings, other bids began coming in. Israel wanted the collection. So did London's Tate Gallery, which offered ten prized acres in Regent's Park as a building site, and us museums from Baltimore to Los Angeles. Nelson Rockefeller, then the governor of New York State, descended upon Hirshhorn, offering $10 million from a state bond issue to build a museum in the town of Purchase, New York, just across the state border from Greenwich. "Well," Ripley later admitted, "my competitive sense was aroused. I felt, as indeed Joe eventually agreed, that the museum in Washington would be more visible and more attended and more for the benefit of all Americans than a museum in Purchase, New York." Hirshhorn had, after all, landed at Ellis Island when he was eleven years old, made his money in America—albeit from investments in Canada— and avowed that he wanted to do "whatever I do for America."[11]

That summer, Ripley was still worrying that the Smithsonian might lose out to Rockefeller, despite all the positive indications. "I feel we are losing ground," he wrote to the influential White House adviser and speechwriter Richard Goodwin. "[Hirshhorn] is in love with his collection. He wants to feel it is as much loved, wherever it lands, as he himself is capable of loving it . . . he needs what I can only describe as cozening, and not direct power or political leverage."[12] Rather than pressure him, Ripley calmly suggested that Hirshhorn to take whatever course he was most comfortable with.

Hesitant as Hirshhorn remained, by November Ripley could report to Mrs. Johnson that Hirshhorn and his curator were "very strongly inclined toward giving the collections to Washington."[13] At last he was able to confirm the offer in a memorandum to the president dated April 26, 1966. Johnson reacted by handing over the project to the highly respected senior White House aide Harry McPherson with instructions to do everything needed to generate legislation providing the site and $14 million in funds to build the Joseph H. Hirshhorn Museum and Sculpture Garden and create the operational and administrative apparatus required.

Accordingly, McPherson and colleagues contacted every member of the House and Senate public works committees, dodging opposition from some opposing the small size and placement of the adjoining sculpture garden and the museum's controversial circular design as presented by Gordon Bunshaft of the well-respected firm of Skidmore, Owings, and Merrill. Ripley had unilaterally chosen him as the project architect without convening a committee or soliciting alternative proposals. Some called into question placing on the prestigious Mall a prominent structure named for a Jewish immigrant to the United States. But Congress shrugged off all such concerns, passing the needed legislation on November 7. Said Ripley, "I felt I had to bulldoze this thing through fast."[14]

Ground was broken on January 1969, after approval had been won from five different federal agencies with permitting responsibilities. The museum opened to the public on October 5, 1974, after great fanfare with eighteen thousand guests over two nights. The *Washington Post*'s Sally Quinn reported that "Hirshhorn disappointed no one with his performance. . . . He demanded a high chair when his turn to speak came, spent much of the evening hugging and kissing and occasionally crying." Even then some laughed at the building's design. The *Washington Post* critic Paul Richard said it was "more intimidating than inviting." The critic Ada Louise Huxtable wrote that Bunshaft's "marble doughnut" had been "born dead," and its design was "neo-penitentiary modern."[15] But Ripley welcomed Bunshaft's deviation from the mediocrity of usual government buildings. And undeniably, Richard continued, the Hirshhorn collection "[is] so rich, so eclectic and inclusive, that it ranks, at birth, as one of few museums capable of tracing the mainstreams, and the tributaries, of the art of the past century."[16]

Fulfilling Ripley's hopes and the president's as well, Richard concluded, the opening of the Hirshhorn Museum "significantly advances Washington's position as a major international center for the study of art."[17] As Ripley himself had put it in selling the project to Hirshhorn's lawyers, "I pointed out to them . . . the fact that by having the government recognize a contemporary art collection it would be a gesture of great moment in the . . . cultural history of Washington, let alone the country, that we accepted modern art as a fulfillment of the art tradition."[18]

Genteel Warfare on the Mall

Big questions about power and control remained open. The Hirshhorn episode marked the onset of tensions between Ripley and the National Gallery of Art that to some observers labeled him not as a profound thinker but as an audacious opportunist. Said Franklin D. Murphy of Los Angeles, the former UCLA chancellor and Times-Mirror Company chair and a National Gallery board member: "Dillon Ripley was the greatest empire builder in the history of Washington. You can see the Mall—it's Dillon Ripley."[19] Friction broke out soon after Ripley's arrival in 1964 and continued until the early 1970s, when both sides helped bring about an unspoken truce.

The act of Congress that established Washington's National Gallery of Art in 1937 specified that it would become a "bureau" of the Smithsonian along with eight other institutions. The Smithsonian's secretary would, ex officio, occupy one of four public seats on the Gallery's board. But if technically the Gallery could be seen as a Smithsonian bureau, its board also included five private or "general" trustees, constituting a majority, and was empowered to be self-perpetuating. With the balance of power in its hands, this group could hire the Gallery's director and deal directly with Congress in setting and managing its budget. Each year a brief summary of Gallery activities would appear in the Smithsonian's annual report, but the Smithsonian lacked the authority to control the nature of these activities. In his memoirs, published in 1992, the president of the Gallery during this period, Paul Mellon, expressed doubt that "anyone these days thinks of the Gallery as being part of that Institution's immense, albeit prestigious bureaucracy."[20]

The relationship worked fine as long as the Smithsonian remained benign and little concerned with art matters. But Ripley's more aggressive approach brought a reaction. With rumors circulating that Ripley wanted to annex the National Gallery, and the Gallery fighting hard to protect its autonomy, its director, John Walker, and president, Paul Mellon, became "quite antagonistic towards myself," said Ripley, "and towards our doing anything positive in the field of art. They felt there was only *one* art museum in Washington. Period. And it should do everything for culture, art, the world . . . and this was a rather hard rock attitude. . . . John Walker in later years told me that he did everything in his power to oppose anything we suggested about the advancement of art and culture for the Smithsonian, because they viewed it as a rival effort to their hegemony." The National Gallery had a "very glacial atmosphere . . . a cloistered atmosphere . . . like a very, very big bank, " Ripley recalled.[21] "You felt that something about the Mellons had traveled all the way from Pittsburgh to Washington to the National Gallery. It was awesome and rather frightening, I think, for some people, and slightly off-putting for me. It just excited my more liberal, more democratic tendencies, so that I would occasionally speak up at the meetings in a way that might make them uncomfortable, but I couldn't help it."[22]

The Smithsonian "was one of the big thorns in John Walker's side," said Elizabeth Foy, his longtime secretary. "He had to fight it tooth and nail. The Smithsonian letterhead at one point, for example, included the National Gallery. . . . Mr. Walker had to fight very hard to get that taken off." Walker saw keeping Ripley at bay as part of his job.[23]

Federal legislation in 1937 created the National Gallery of Art as a home for the splendid Andrew W. Mellon collection of European-focused fine arts. It also provided for the establishment of a new museum, then called the National Collection of Fine Arts (NCFA) to house several other Smithsonian-owned collections of American art that had been out of public view for many years. The National Portrait Gallery, modeled after the London equivalent, had been founded in 1921 but still lacked a home of its own.

In 1962, Congress voted to establish the National Portrait Gallery as a separate Smithsonian bureau to honor men and women who have made significant contributions to the United States. It and the NCFA—retitled the National Museum of American Art in 1980 and renamed the Smithsonian American Art Museum (SAAM) in 2000—would share the historic and spacious Old Patent Office Building near the Mall, thus saving it from demolition to make way for a parking lot. Ripley interpreted the legislation to mean that this museum should aspire to "collect modern American art, contemporary American art . . . and to create within the framework of the national collection a continuing interpretation of American art." Soon after arrival, then, Ripley felt he had a green light to improve the Smithsonian's position in the art field, and physical space to allocate to the effort.

Before proceeding very far, Ripley found himself faced with an internal obstacle: the extreme conservatism of the NCFA's governing body. Its chair, Paul Manship, said Ripley, was a "charming person" but "very slow and very antagonistic toward anything modern" and "sort of a no man." At the first meeting of the NCFA commission that Ripley attended, Manship reacted with horror at the idea of acquiring a small, benign John Marin watercolor and had to be overruled. He eventually retired, leaving the way open for a new NCFA director to be brought in. Ripley's choice was the Harvard-trained art historian David Scott, who arrived with ample energy and many apparently good ideas.[24]

Scott was credited by Paul Richard as having "transformed the National Collection of Fine Arts from a tiny and neglected Government bureau into a major Washington museum."[25] But, said Richard, Scott's hope to achieve a great collection at the NCFA had been stymied, on one hand, by the powerful National Gallery and, on the other, by the Hirshhorn acquisition. Ripley had created the impasse. Complaining that Scott "was not as innovative and stylish and creative as I had anticipated," Ripley corrected the situation by firing him.[26] As his successor, he brought in the prominent University of Chicago art historian Joshua Taylor. Thus he signaled greater interest in scholarship than in other art museum activities. Known for his gentle erudition, Taylor singlehandedly did much to improve the Smithsonian–National Gallery relationship. Scott went on to a successful late-career move to the National Gallery before he retired.

A separate issue had to do with where to place the formidable sculptures that were prominent in both collections. Keen to have a sculpture park on the Mall, Ripley proposed a large cross-mall site extending northward from Jefferson Drive to Constitution Avenue. To Ripley's surprise, the Gallery countered with a plan to found a national sculpture garden along Pennsylvania Avenue, between the National Gallery and the National Museum of Natural History. The park would be jointly administered by the Gallery and the National Park Service, manager of the Mall. It would form part of the lower Pennsylvania Avenue development initiative that was then taking shape.

Debate over the merits of these proposals continued for years. Neither side emerged as a clear victor. The Smithsonian ended up with a small recessed sculpture park for the Hirshhorn, not extending across the Mall and unable to display more work than Hirshhorn could comfortably install at his own garden in Greenwich. Ripley had to counter Hirshhorn's complaints of having been buried and, like Tutankhamun, "discovered in my tomb." After years of discussions, the National Gallery in 1999 finally opened its own handsome 6.1-acre sculpture park along Constitution Avenue adjacent to the Gallery's west building. Featuring works by such artists as Claes Oldenburg and David Smith, the garden has a fountain that becomes a popular skating rink in cold weather. The elegant J. Carter Brown, who in 1969 succeeded Walker as the National Gallery's director, would have, like Ripley, preferred model sailboats in the style of the Tuileries.

In 1970, the Smithsonian acquired the massive Archives of American Art, founded in 1954 by the art historian E. P. Richardson, which the *Washington Post* called "a major center for the scholarly study of the history of American art."[27] This field had long been ignored in favor of scholarship having to do with more fashionable European art. With this new Smithsonian bureau in place and a new Center for Advanced Study in the Visual Arts, planned as a principal feature of the National Gallery's East Building to open in 1978, Washington's ranking as a focal point for art scholarship was on a rapid rise. So were the prospects for rivalry between two major new scholarly institutions.

Petty matters sometimes provoked friction. For the academic procession during the 1965 Smithson bicentennial, Ripley wanted the president of the National Gallery, Paul Mellon, to march wearing Smithsonian robes as a representative of one of its bureaus. Mellon refused amid acrimony and marched, sporting Oxford red, with the Yale University delegation. In his book *Reflections in a Silver Spoon*, Mellon chided Ripley, claiming he "had been overcome with theatrical ambitions, or had at least been infected with mild institutional euphoria," and added that he had "no intention" of allowing Gallery representatives to follow Ripley's parade instructions. Ripley, Mellon continued, was "not very pleased."[28] When Ripley's schedule compelled him to skip some Gallery board meetings, the Gallery consistently rebuffed his efforts to send Charles Blitzer as his representative. That was elitism, Ripley complained, though many boards do not permit such substitutions. Ripley was also criticized for introducing the "very daring and dangerous" practice of serving cocktails at dinner in Smithsonian art exhibition spaces. "But what if someone threw a martini into a Matisse?" asked one alarmed Gallery official.[29]

For his part, Ripley "never could quite get used to the inherent sense of competitiveness" at the Gallery and felt a "sense of austerity and cold elitism" that stood out in contrast to his own "more liberal and democratic tendencies." A visit to the Gallery made him feel that he was entering the "cloistered atmosphere" of a "very, very big bank" with green marble floors. "The Gallery had decided to divorce itself as much as possible from the Smithsonian," he said.

> If they had decided that, they ought to rest easy. . . they could choose to ignore it. But it seemed to get under their skin that the Smithsonian existed, and that it was . . . active and doing a lot of things, and therefore competitive. . . .
>
> I think that they objected to the fact that I attempted to make the Smithsonian better known in Washington. And the public in Washington involves, of course, a kind of political atmosphere which everyone has to be conscious of and attempt to work with. They were afraid that I might be stealing some of their chestnuts. Because if you get important Senators or Congressmen or, God knows what, high muckamucks to come to a function opening at the Smithsonian, that might detract by an iota from the ever present drive of the National Gallery to have first place."[30]

In this climate, Ripley added, "I would occasionally speak up at the meetings in a way that might make them uncomfortable." Charles Blitzer did what he could to avoid conflict and maneuver the Smithsonian toward what in 1970 he called "a very good position to hold our own in the face of the National Gallery's masterpieces and wealth." In a sharply worded memorandum, Blitzer said why. While the Gallery was busily constructing its new East Building, an I. M. Pei masterpiece, the Smithsonian could take pride in having assembled a first-class team of art museum directors. And the Archives of American Art acquisition improved Ripley's competitive position.[31]

Ripley was sometimes tempted to position the Smithsonian at the apex of Washington's emerging greatness as a world-class art center and to relegate the National Gallery to a lesser, specialized role. The suave and highly effective J. Carter Brown smoothly countered these moves, concealing his ambition to become Washington's minister of culture. With his own sharp tongue, which matched Ripley's wit, Brown wryly noted Ripley's "rather dynamic" view of the Smithsonian.

Eventually, the key players on both sides cooled off. Even for the super-dexterous Ripley, just running the Smithsonian was quite a handful, and he came to accept the reality that the NCFA would remain "a lesser gallery in competition with the National Gallery." He said he regretted the antagonism: "I felt very badly about this, because I felt that it was not in the tradition." Ripley also came to recognize that despite his frustrations and occasional outbursts at National Gallery board meetings, they were "one family." And whatever differences he and Brown had over official or policy matters, the two eminently clubbable men moved in the same genteel, upper

Ivy League social circles more accustomed to civility than to power struggles. "We lunch occasionally in Washington, and there are no echoes of our contretemps of many years ago," wrote Mellon in *Reflections in a Silver Spoon*.[32]

As Walker neared retirement in 1969, relations between the two also improved. Replacing what Elizabeth Foy recalled as "a decided standoffishness between the two," they became "very friendly" in later years. In a letter to Ripley dated October 10, 1969, Carter Brown noted "all the ways in which we are lucky to be a bureau of the Smithsonian," pointing out "how clairvoyant Andrew Mellon had been in not letting us become an unprotected morsel floating about ready to be gobbled up by any alphabetical agency or bureaucratic unit that might be feeling hungry. Not only lucky but proud too."[33]

Mellon's book notes that the National Gallery–Smithsonian relationship had mellowed in the aftermath of the bicentennial celebrations, becoming "smooth, businesslike, and cordial," and that he and Ripley had "become fast friends and sincere admirers of each other." Carter Brown's father, the New England blueblood John Nicholas Brown, was a stalwart Smithsonian board member of long standing. Family ties helped keep relations civil. So did the fact that Ripley was keeping himself plenty busy elsewhere on the Mall and beyond.

CHAPTER SEVEN

Media Ventures and
Scholarly Triumph

In the 1960s, with television manifesting huge audiences and print media still powerful forces, it is no wonder that Dillon Ripley was attracted to the mass communications field even though it was intensely competitive. At the same time, he sought ways to establish the Smithsonian as a high-brow institution as well as a popular voice. His success at both these levels, as well as in the field of personal interactions between famous people, marked him for innovation and insight as a master communicator.

Seldom one to shun the spotlight, Ripley began dabbling with various film and television ideas soon after World War II. Periodically during his Yale years and later at the Smithsonian, there were discussions about radio programs and some experiments. A National Geographic film crew came along on the Smithsonian/Yale/National Geographic Society's 1949 expedition into Nepal that Ripley led. The team produced an hour-long color film featuring both the exotic pageantry of the seldom-visited capital and scenes from the expedition's excursions into the backcountry up to the edge of Mount Everest and other Himalayan peaks. The film was widely seen early in 1951 during a sixteen-stop lecture tour in the United States arranged by a lecture management company, with Ripley billed as a noted naturalist-explorer and a rising star.

Soon after, Ripley appeared as a guest on an award-winning Sunday evening CBS quiz show called *What in the World*, in which panels of experts recruited by the University of Pennsylvania's anthropology museum would identify and discuss objects from various distant places. "The manner in which the panel, confronted with the various objects, without clues as to their origin beyond their own knowledge and training," Ripley reported, "manage to identify, discuss, and enlarge informally about these things, has apparently constantly fascinated and intrigued vary large audiences."[1]

A similar Yale venture into educational TV could effectively promote Yale's Peabody Museum and science, he felt. In several 1952 letters, he pitched the idea to prospective sponsors, including Yale's well-heeled Lefty Lewis. The project got nowhere, with faculty members arguing that they lacked the time for such frivolity. In October 1966, the Smithsonian did launch a Sunday afternoon TV series as a joint venture with NBC. Sandwiched between talk shows and football games, the show did not last long. But Ripley's enthusiasm for such initiatives marked his fervent interest in disseminating knowledge to broad audiences.

A TV series called *Smithsonian World*, with the engaging historian David McCullough as host and Ripley as an occasional guest, ran weekly on public television for six seasons starting in 1984. It was way too late for Ripley, who would retire that year, to become seriously involved. The series mixed segments on scientific research and environmental conservation with arts and humanities content aimed at a popular audience.

With regard to print media, no one at the Smithsonian knew much about publishing or editing a national magazine for the general public. Competition was stiffening. Still, it became common knowledge that what Ripley most keenly wanted was a magazine. A print publication would do much to put the Smithsonian on the map for people all over the nation, not just visitors to Washington. It would expedite the growth of the Institution's influence and align with founder James Smithson's instruction that his gift to the United States be used to diffuse knowledge as well as to increase it. Ripley felt that a Smithsonian magazine project was way overdue and should have been initiated early in the 1900s. He had seen a place for "a magazine of Man and what affects him . . . his environment, sciences, arts, adventures, follies, fortunes." He assigned his "righthand handyman," William Warner, a gifted author who later won a Pulitzer Prize for his stirring book *Beautiful Swimmers* about the blue crabs of the Chesapeake, to the task of fleshing out the idea.

Warner's initial research led to an encounter in 1968 between Ripley and the talented editor Edward K. Thompson, a North Dakota native who early in his newspaper career had become known for his skill at using pictures to help tell stories. In 1937, the rough-hewn Thompson left the *Milwaukee Journal* to join the fledgling *Life* magazine as a photo editor. He then nurtured *Life*, long the flagship of Henry R. Luce's Time Inc. empire, working there for thirty years, eighteen of them as *Life*'s editor or managing editor.

Thompson's style differed sharply from that of the more frequently encountered Ivy Leaguers populating the company. *Life*'s Philip Kunhardt described him as a "feisty, hard-nosed, sentimental intellectual in hick's clothing."[2] With "his hair slicked back, his tie loosened, swearing a lot, and a fat cigar in his mouth," recalled the writer and editor Carey Winfrey, he found "a lotta foofaw" abroad in the world.[3] "He looked like a hog butcher, but he was one of the few geniuses I've ever been close to in my life," wrote Timothy Foote, another longtime editorial colleague.[4]

Thompson carried on with brilliant success as a print journalist until Big Television started clipping the general magazines' wings in the 1960s. Top employees suffered even at mighty *Life*. In 1967, Luce died. After thirty years of working for him, Thompson was told by his successor, Hedley Donovan, that "it was time for a change" and that another company veteran, Thomas Griffith, would become *Life*'s editor. Thompson, conceding that Donovan was entitled to choose his own team, was kicked upstairs with an opportunity to become director of editorial services. The position would have been "an honorable one, to be sure," he wrote in his memoirs, but after sleeping on it he chose retirement over the lesser job.[5]

"Upon leaving *Life* I didn't expect—and didn't get—a flood of job offers," Thompson wrote. "At equal pay, I was priced out of the job market." He did receive a feeler from William P. Bundy, assistant secretary of state for Southeast Asian affairs and Secretary of State Dean Acheson's son-in-law, as to whether he might be willing to help explain the Vietnam War to an increasingly testy US public. His patriotic instincts aroused, Thompson accepted, moved from New York to Washington, and set forth on this quixotic crusade. Disillusionment soon set in. Thompson was especially dismayed when he discovered that General William Westmoreland, who commanded all US military operations in Vietnam from 1964 to 1968, was making the same claims in top-secret reports to his superiors in Washington and to the media in the field. As he grew increasingly angry about Vietnam as well, Thompson found himself clearly "in the wrong pew" and resigned in the fall of 1968.[6] At age sixty-two, he was very available.

Founding Smithsonian *Magazine*

The Smithsonian executive William Warner invited Thompson to lunch, quizzed him about how to launch a magazine, and floated some sample story ideas. These did not pass muster with Thompson. But the lunch did set the stage for a memorable weekend in Litchfield, where Thompson and Ripley sat under a tree, with a downy woodpecker tap-tapping above them, to sketch out the possible *Smithsonian* magazine of which Thompson would become publisher as well as editor. The event marked the beginning of what Thompson called "a rewarding relationship, professional and personal." He found Ripley to "have an aristocratic manner but also to be both engagingly self-deprecatory and most articulate."[7]

At the outset of their talks, even though what Thompson termed "death rattles" were emanating from prominent general magazines like *Look*, the *Saturday Evening Post*, and even *Life*, Thompson saw hope in some quarters. "If there was no longer a mass market for a magazine that was everything to everyone," he said, "there might be a substantial opportunity for one that could do what nothing but a magazine could do." He and Ripley quickly rejected the notion that the new magazine could be a house organ, covering only the work of the Smithsonian's bureaus. "A magazine confined to what the Institution had on view, including temporary shows," he told Warner, "would run out of editorial material in a very short time. The turnover on the painstakingly fashioned exhibits was slow. I was wary and not at all interested in the kind of official publications that most other institutions were offering."[8] That option disposed of, the two then began to pencil in their thoughts about what the magazine could do.

They forged what would over the long term become a succinct mission statement—that the content of their "unmagazine" would be "whatever the Institution was interested in, or might be interested in," or should be interested in. "That was about all that was articulated as a working idea," Thompson said, but an almost unlimited variety of subject matter was possible under such a concept.[9] Years later, the Smithsonian crafted a formal mission statement for the magazine, stating the banal truth that learning never ends and describing the magazine's content in terms less persuasive than what Ripley and Thompson had cooked up.

Thompson soon won Ripley's agreement that he would have "a free hand in giving shape to the magazine." Total independence turned out to be an elusive goal, for Ripley frequently sent Thompson instructions as to what he wanted published. But the two men shared similar general ideas about the magazine, which would be aimed at a well-educated and affluent audience. Avoiding the preparation of a slick prospectus, Thompson put together some general thoughts about what it would encompass:

> [It] would be based on, but I hoped ahead of, the country's rising educational level. It would spur on the upward movement encouraged by the GI Bill. It would spur curiosity in already receptive minds. It would deal with history as it is relevant to the present. It would present art, since true art is never dated, in the richest possible reproduction. It would peer into

the future via coverage of social progress and of science and technology. Technical matters would be digested and made intelligible by skilled writers who would stimulate readers to reach upward while not turning them off with jargon. We would find the best writers and the best photographers—not unlike the best of the old *Life*.[10]

In January 1969, Thompson sent Ripley a memorandum summarizing his thoughts about the project. He rejected the idea of a bimonthly or quarterly publication, which would be "an adornment to the institution" but would lack the punch of a monthly schedule, which would do far more to make the magazine "habit-forming for both readers and advertisers."[11] A *Time*-sized magazine on glossy paper ($8\frac{1}{2} \times 11\frac{1}{8}$ inches) would be large enough to showcase top-quality four-color photographs but offer savings in the paper and production costs of a larger format. The use of the Institution's name as the magazine's title would signal its prestige.

The memorandum provided some samples of the kinds of articles to be featured and identified a few editors and assistants who might form a skeleton staff. By May, Thompson had become far more specific about editorial content, agreeing with Ripley about "wrapping the magazine around the theme of man . . . what environment does to modern man . . . and what he does to his environment, so we can have lots of cute little threatened beasties."[12] For the first issue's lead article, he scheduled what became an "eloquent and witty treatment by renowned biologist René Dubos of the give-and-take between man and his environment."[13]

While Ripley and Thompson had sharpened their opinions about the editorial content of their "un-magazine," there was no certainty about the source of the funding needed to launch it. Ripley as usual felt that a good idea would somehow attract money. But Congress would surely not pay the initial bills as part of its annual Smithsonian appropriation. Ripley had violated Smithsonian tradition by seeking private money for some of his ventures to supplement often insufficient federal funding. But he and his deputies could not pinpoint any easy source of private support for the magazine.

The Institution's treasurer, Ames Wheeler, a former steel executive from Pittsburgh, steadfastly opposed the idea of private funding and urged Ripley to abandon it. "Go to hell, Ames," Ripley said, urging Thompson to carry on. The cost of launching other new magazines, *Psychology Today* for example, reached heights of $5 million or more. All Ripley could claim for Smithsonian was $5,000 from William Benton toward a possible joint venture with his *Encyclopaedia Britannica*. Allegedly, though IBM could not confirm this when queried, there was also a $50,000 gift from IBM's Thomas Watson. In his memoirs, Thompson cites a newspaper article in which Ripley was quoted as stating that Watson, a birdwatcher, had pledged to underwrite losses if the project collapsed. But at the time that was not known to Thompson or his staff. "I might have felt more confident if I had known about that safety net," said Thompson, "but I spent no time on iffy speculation, only on making the magazine a critical and a financial success."[14]

Office space in the old Arts and Industries Building was scarce, and what there was of it was situated in poorly ventilated former storage areas where some sweaty magazine workers doubled or quadrupled up. One editor, Edwards Park, as quoted in the magazine's thirty-fifth anniversary issue, dated November 2005, said that working conditions were primitive: "We were moved all over the place. There was one interior storage room where four of us ended up—staring at walls without windows, gasping for oxygen." Inevitably it was dubbed the Black Hole. One claustrophobe moved out of it and placed his desk directly outside the editor's office to serve as a haunting prod to the administrative conscience. Park changed offices nineteen times during the pioneer years, he recalled.[15] Ripley visited the dank premises. "How quaint," he murmured.

Under such unpromising circumstances, the staff spent 1969 preparing and publishing a charter issue of *Smithsonian*, as the magazine was titled. It was dated April 1970, and it came out on the basis of the regents' guarded approval—at one key moment the *Washington Post* did not help by wrongly reporting that they had dropped the project—and a little front money that Wheeler reluctantly coughed up to keep it afloat until subscription revenues began coming in. Handsomely illustrated articles in the charter issue featured a range of subjects, from elephant training in Ceylon to art treasures at New York's Metropolitan Museum of Art, black studies in Maryland, and human overpopulation.

Positive reactions came quickly from old pros such as *Life*'s Tom Griffith, Thompson's successor, who found "no look of trial and error or slapdash about it."[16] Each issue, reported an admiring *Newsweek*, "is convincing evidence that eye-popping layouts, superb color photography and solid craftsmanship will always lure an audience."[17] There were complaints from Smithsonian scientists who felt that the magazine should feature their research, but Thompson and Ripley disdainfully ignored that sort of parochialism.

Financially, what won the day for the magazine was its close relationship with the Smithsonian Associates program that had become popular in Washington. Already in Ripley's reign, the local Associates program had attracted some 9,000 members, who enjoyed special activities and benefits. In 1969, 3 million people received invitations to become charter national associates, with the new magazine as the principal benefit. Only associates would get the magazine, which would not be sold on newsstands. Fees would vary from ten dollars for an individual to twenty dollars for a family. National Geographic Society membership, whose principal benefit is its magazine, was a model. For the Smithsonian the concept worked famously well, quickly attracting 160,000 charter subscribers. The magazine's circulation climbed steadily upward, reaching a million in 1975 and a remarkable peak of 2,131,660 in 1995.

Never except during the very early days, Thompson said proudly in his memoirs, did the Institution "have to spend any actual cash on us—our cash flow was always positive." Subscriptions held steady, said Tom Ott of Smithsonian Enterprises, "at a time when audiences were being challenged in the era of digitization and exploding options."[18] These results were achieved without newsstand sales and without assembling the large advertising sales and circulation promotion staffs in the free-spending manner of the *National Geographic* and some other magazines. Ripley awarded Thompson the Joseph Henry Medal, the Institution's highest honor. In an unusual editorial misstep, Ripley handed him a citation that sent mixed signals, complimenting the editor for being "dauntless in purpose and rarely persuasive." Asked Thompson, "Did that mean that I wasn't persuasive very often?"

Persuasive indeed was the rumpled Thompson, whose skills as an editor are often compared to those of H. L. Mencken at the *American Mercury* or Harold Ross at the *New Yorker*.

Much of the project's success also stemmed from the talents of the editors who succeeded Thompson after his ten-year stint and worked hard to preserve his style and legacy. His first successor, the *Life* alumnus Don Moser, lasted twenty years. Moser was known for uncompromisingly high standards, avoidance of trendy stories about celebrities, and an uncanny ability to "surprise" readers by offering them material that, reported the *Washington Post*, "they had seen nowhere else and were unlikely to see in the future."[19]

Moser's successor, Carey Winfrey, there for another decade, was struck by how consistently the magazine had remained aligned with what Thompson had envisioned, what he and Moser had fashioned, and what Ripley had the nerve to assemble. Though Moser tried to make *Smithsonian* "a bit more topical," Winfrey wrote, he remained loyal to the idea that his well-educated readers wanted "thoughtful — even challenging — journalism about history, nature, science and the arts. And stunning photography. And a dollop of wit now and then."[20]

Memorializing Woodrow Wilson

While the magazine appealed to a broad readership, Ripley also fastened his gaze upon academics at the highest level. He started off with scant respect for Washington's scholarly institutions. "The general climate in the early 1960s," he whispered, was not one in which higher education was held in great esteem in Washington. There were at least four universities, and yet the consensus among academics was that none of them was really in the first rank."[21] Though the situation would greatly improve later on, Ripley added, it was in the 1980s still commonly felt that "the international aspects of higher education and the post-doctoral levels of higher education in Washington remained uneven and tended to be slightly, at least, deficient, although voluble arguments would ensue if I were to make such a statement in public."[22]

When Ripley left Yale for Washington, one of his dreams was to help correct this shortcoming by establishing at the Smithsonian a "small department or a small entity that would narrow the gap between Yale's high scholarly standards and those he found in Washington. This small unit would take a broader view than several existing think tanks, would especially address international aspects at the topmost levels of postdoctoral scholarship and research, and would avoid "dipping into the field of political science," where Washington was already strong. It "would be involved in many, if not all, the interests of the Institution itself, whether in the fields of history, biology, or art history."[23] It would avoid overlap with the respected Brookings Institution, where high-level government officials would camp out between political appointments, and scores of other think tanks. Distinguished scholars from all over the world would be invited to work on their projects.

Once locked into his postdoctoral idea, Ripley as usual exercised all of his wiles, digging deep into his network, to make it happen. Often, in status-conscious Washington, aspirants to power decorate their offices with signed photos of national leaders and make exaggerated use of the phrase "He's a great personal friend of mine." Ripley had no need to employ such excesses of verbal conflation. In Washington as elsewhere, he was already an insider. As an initial step toward the realization of his postdoc dream, Ripley assigned his principal deputy, Assistant Secretary Charles Blitzer, to conduct some sleuthing in the archives and in the halls of Congress. A liberal political scientist who had taught at Yale, the New School, and the City University of New York, Blitzer had also spent time at the American Council of Learned Societies, the Phi Beta Kappa organization, and the National Commission on the Humanities, and in his own right was a well-known fixture in academia.

Blitzer's digging revealed that the time was right for the nation to bring into being a memorial honoring the scholarly former US president Woodrow Wilson. The Congress had long since created a Woodrow Wilson Memorial Commission to study the matter and recommend something suitable. Named as its chair was Wilson's grandson, Francis Bowes Sayre, dean of the National Cathedral. But the commission had done nothing, Blitzer found: "Dean Sayre was so vehemently unhappy about the Vietnam War that—since we were now in the Johnson Administration—he refused ever to have the commission meet or to have anything to do with anything that was in any way official. . . . He wasn't going to be playing ball with the United States government, even to memorialize his grandfather."[24]

Prompted by Blitzer, Sayre at last relented and set up hearings to study the matter. One of Sayre's commissioners was the New Jersey veteran Congress member Peter Frelinghuysen, who along with his wife were good friends of Mary Ripley's. There was a consensus at the time, Ripley recalled, that Woodrow Wilson was not the sort of person who would be easy to commemorate with "a mounted equestrian statue, in full uniform in the style of General Ulysses Grant or these other military heroes." More appropriate, he felt, would be to have the scholarly Wilson "striding along in academic dress." More important was the idea that a *living* memorial to Wilson could be created with a far greater emphasis on ideas and words than on bricks and mortar or statuary.[25]

Invited by Frelinghuysen to testify on the Hill, Blitzer helped Ripley by stating that "we wanted to see an institution developed in the District of Columbia which would be for post-graduate studies, would be international in the spirit of Woodrow Wilson, and would be quite different from the existing institutions." Its focus would be not on straight political history, but rather on cultural, scientific, and ecological considerations. Its mandate, it was finally decided, should address both the broad issues that Ripley had been championing, working toward "symbolizing and strengthening the fruitful relation between the world of learning and the world of public affairs. Ripley proclaimed that scholars at the proposed institution would undertake two general areas of study: the international law of the sea and the broad aspects of social biology. Initial studies, he added, would lead toward "many of the scholarly workings of the Institution itself."[26]

The plan met with some opposition from within the Smithsonian, where Ripley had difficulty "getting many of my dear colleagues on the science side to be in the least interested in the environment. It seemed that the museum people had to be woken up to the fact that their own resources were shrinking even as they were making their studies."[27] But with Peter Frelinghuysen's help on the Hill and that of Wilson scholars, who stated that the idea would not conflict with existing Wilson memorials, the idea got a thumbs-up from both houses of Congress. President Johnson, said Ripley, was "a history buff and very much concerned about establishing, in parity if not superiority, his role as an intellectual with that of his late predecessor." An early champion of the idea, LBJ proclaimed in a

1965 speech his support for "Secretary Ripley's dream of creating here on the Mall a great center for scholars" and signed on with no argument to the necessary legislation.[28] Washington's Woodrow Wilson International Center for Scholars, much as Ripley and Blitzer had conceived it, was founded and began to function in 1968.

Its first home was on the third floor of the Smithsonian Castle. It was "symbolic of the activities to which that building was dedicated in the formative years of the Smithsonian," Ripley said, "that we should now have advanced scholars concerned with common themes of study housed in the red sandstone castle on the Mall."[29] Ripley became a charter member of its fifteen-person board. The former senator Daniel Patrick Moynihan, another personal friend of the Ripleys, did much to design the Center. Efforts were made to enhance its prestige by equipping it with its own building, as an increment of Moynihan's Pennsylvania Avenue redevelopment project, but ultimately these failed. Later, from 1988 to 1997, Charles Blitzer served as its director, masterminding its move from the Castle to much improved quarters in the massive Ronald Reagan Building on Pennsylvania Avenue near the Mall.

Ripley had hoped that the Wilson Center would fold into the Smithsonian as another of its bureaus. But he had "stuck into a thorny bed," Ripley confessed, when it came to the question of who would be in charge. Ripley hoped that the Smithsonian's regents would be empowered to appoint Wilson Center board members. Ripley had encouraged Blitzer, who helped draft the legislation, to work closely with Moynihan and "make sure this comes out as part of the Smithsonian." But during the detailed discussions about the legislation, two members of the White House staff, Harry McPherson and

Douglass Cater, insisted that a majority of its directors be appointed by the president. Said Ripley:

> That pretty well insured the fact that Doug Cater wanted to make it autonomous, in the spirit of the National Gallery or the Kennedy Center, so that it would not be, in effect, a creature of the Smithsonian. That disappointed me, because my initial ambition, which I'm sure was boundless, was that it should be part and parcel of the Smithsonian and another very superior bureau, one that we would be immensely proud of in the future. But no, I lost on that one.[30]

The reason for the White House's opposition, recalled Blitzer in an oral history interview, was apprehension on the part of the former president of Brown University, Barnaby Keeney, then serving as chair of the National Endowment for the Humanities. He "did not trust me and he did not trust Dillon Ripley, and thought . . . this was going to be some great power grab. But despite some headaches, principally difficulties in selecting some of the presidential appointees to the board and inattention to their needs once aboard," Blitzer said that overall the relationship worked smoothly.[31]

In 1980, the Wilson Center got a major boost with the arrival on the premises of the iconic Soviet Union scholar and diplomat George Kennan, sponsor of the idea that US interests would be better served by "containing" the Soviets rather than confronting them. Ripley had persuaded him to station himself and his considerable entourage and grant monies at the Center rather than at Brookings or Johns Hopkins University's School of Advanced International Studies. The Kennan group's arrival has helped the Wilson Center maintain high scholarly standards. Staff leadership has been distinguished. The *Wilson Quarterly*, a scholarly publication that now appears only on the Web, has earned high marks. High-ranking fellows flock to the Center from all over the world at the rate of about 150 a year. They write, analyze, and discuss, framing issues for decision- and policymakers in truly constructive and nonpartisan dialogue.

Perhaps in reaction to his inability to control the Wilson Center, which he had designed, Ripley moved fast to energize the Smithsonian's own ability to arrange scholarly seminars and symposia. To put them together, he engaged the anthropologist Wilton Dillon (no relative), a Margaret Mead protégé. As the Smithsonian's director of symposia and seminars and for a while as a Wilson Center guest scholar, Dillon helped organize gatherings on broad topics that, as Ripley put it, intersected with both institutions. A practitioner of what Dillon called intellectual show business, he did his best to lure visitors up to his handsomely furnished office in the Smithsonian Castle's South Tower. He made it into what he called a veritable salon attracting a broad range of distinguished visitors from many lands and fields. There, on one notable occasion, he and his guest, the actress Elizabeth Taylor, toasted James Smithson with glasses of Virginia Gentleman whiskey.

Along the way, as the recently deceased Wilton Dillon says in his book *Smithsonian Stories*, his office tried hard to satisfy Ripley's cravings for brainy discussions of big topics. The symposium series began with a 1965 gathering entitled "Knowledge Among Men," a celebration honoring the 200th anniversary of James Smithson's birth. Other broadly titled events included "The Nature of Scientific Discovery" (1973) and, honoring the US Bicentennial, "The United States and the World" (1976). An especially celebrated occasion was a well-attended symposium entitled "Man and Beast," which

explored the implications of human efforts to subjugate nature and was, according to Ripley, a "fine escape from an-
thropocentrism." "There are many things that other creatures
from ants to birds to baboons can tell us, which can serve as
guides along the way to knowing ourselves," Ripley said. A
broad question he raised was "How can we learn enough about
ourselves to stop in time?"[32] Another grandly titled gathering
was "The Fitness of Man's Environment" (1967), one of many
Ripley efforts to direct much-needed official attention toward
pressing global environmental issues.

Wilton Dillon remained onstage, peddling his special brand
of what he called "intellectual popcorn in the big Smithsonian
circus tent," from the late 1960s to 1989, when the curtain
rang down and he was driven away by the post-Ripley bureaucracy. During his time in office, much knowledge had been
acquired and diffused. Some of the discussions he sponsored
bored Ripley as much as the three tiresome days he had once
spent in Aspen thinking about museums. But he had learned
something about exercising the Smithsonian's power to convene such events.

In a further nod to top academic levels, Blitzer in 1966 created the Smithsonian Council, a visiting committee composed
of twenty-five distinguished scholars and intellectuals with a
mandate to dig deeply into the Institution's complex structure
and proffer advice. This committee met twice a year, and at
each meeting the work and plans of two Smithsonian bureaus
were reviewed. Its reports, sometimes very critical, included
one that, according to the American Antiquarian Society in
its Blitzer obituary, briefed Ripley on a sensitive topic: the
National Zoo's failure to mention the subject of evolution.
Because of the members' high standing, its recommendation

that this omission be corrected carried considerable weight. The Council's outside reviews were taken very seriously by the Smithsonian staff, even though in later years before the Council's demise it was all too often reduced to discussing fundraising issues.

Ripley had worked with great success to extend the Smith-sonian's reach with a daring popular magazine. He had also elevated the Institution's brow with the creation of scholarly opportunities for academics from many fields. Here were further examples of Ripley's restless mind achieving lasting and tangible results.

CHAPTER EIGHT

Building Smithsonian U.

J ust being the voice of the Smithsonian, the world's largest museum complex with 140 million objects in its collections, was by no means enough for Dillon Ripley. Nor
was it good enough just to use those collections to awaken
thought and discussion. He also wanted the Institution to be
as similar as possible, physically as well as intellectually, to a
top-ranking university. The theater in him made him yearn
for robed academic processions whenever possible. And he
wanted a defined physical space.

He felt that museums were "the principal unrecognized
arms of education."[1] He wanted curators to play key parts in
conducting experimental biology research, and thought they
deserved faculty rankings equal to those awarded to university
professors. In 1966, he proposed to the US Congress the passage of a national museum act to underscore the importance of
museums. The Smithsonian and its scholars were, he felt, as
entitled to their own campus workplace as any academicians.

Joseph Henry, the Smithsonian's first secretary, who remained in office from 1846 to 1878, fought hard against the
very idea of having a museum building at all. He felt it would
drain resources away from the publications and scholarly
exchanges that he saw as the principal means of fulfilling

the Institution's mission. Ripley saw the museum as playing a forcefully active educational role. He advocated broad
programs of research and public education, similar to those
available at some other museums, to accompany more traditionally museum-like activities. He also sought to achieve a
truly international voice for the Smithsonian, giving ample
space for regions and cultures to which museums had often
given short shrift.

Soon after his arrival, Ripley began using the Institution's
annual report as a testing ground for ideas. Each issue's opening "Statement by the Secretary" was where he could float
pieces of a broad agenda combining his push for new and
stimulating ideas with an ongoing quest for the physical plant
needed to develop and ventilate them. The "View from the
Castle" column in *Smithsonian* magazine, which Ripley wrote
monthly for many years, was an alternate platform. These were
no mere exercises in empire building on his part. The Smithsonian desperately needed space for its fast-growing array of
people, activities, and collections.

Ripley sent an especially strong early signal of his academic intentions in September 1965, when the Smithsonian
celebrated the bicentennial year of James Smithson's birth
with elaborate pageantry. Star performances, Ripley noted,
included a "robed procession of nearly five hundred delegates
of universities and kindred scholarly institutions, preceded by
our mace bearer and banners of the various Smithsonian bureaus."[2] The jeweled mace had been fashioned in consultation
with the Worshipful Company of Goldsmiths in London. The
Institution's accompanying flag aptly featured the Smithsonian's symbol: a demi-lion holding the sun in its paws. A Marine Corps band performed a trumpet fanfare and other music
composed for the occasion. Further ceremonies included an

elaborate dinner at the Museum of History and Technology, a White House reception, and the bestowing of various Smithsonian medals on selected dignitaries. As was his habit, Ripley previewed the meal before giving the caterer a thumbs-up.

A highlight of the three-day celebration was a scholarly symposium, the first of many such events that Ripley would convene, entitled "Knowledge Among Men." Speakers included Lewis Mumford, Sir Kenneth Clark, Arthur Koestler, Evelyn Hutchinson, and the French anthropologist Claude Lévi-Strauss, famous for his pioneering research among indigenous groups in the Brazilian hinterlands. He issued a ringing challenge to the assembled company: "The day will come when the last primitive culture will have disappeared from the earth, compelling us to realize only too late that the fundamentals of mankind are irretrievably lost," Lévi-Strauss said. He implored his audience to treasure what Ripley called the "seeds of invaluable comparative research on man's ability to survive the disorders of this age"[3] and give "absolute priority" to studying the "so-called primitive peoples," urging researchers to "salvage ethnographic records before they too become extinct."[4]

Years later, in one of his final summations of his Smithsonian career, Ripley would heartily endorse the intellectual globalism that Lévi-Strauss had posited and make a major new effort to counter Americans' lack of understanding of other cultures and societies. "For the first time in our history," he stated,

> we are embarking in a spirit of social responsibility on a creative effort to increase understanding and respect for our neighbors. . . . We can, for example, tell Americans about their history, but how can we extend . . . that to the rest of the world? Traditions and cultures alien to the massive onslaughts

of mechanistic technology are fragile indeed. They are being eroded every day just as the forests of the tropics disappear. Cultures drift away like the dust that follows the draft of a lifting jet plane on a far-away runway.[5]

As Ripley's scholarly preferences grew firmer late in the 1960s, he began to piece together a plan to house them, calling for a spanking-new Smithsonian campus extending southward from the old Smithsonian Castle and the Arts and Industries Building. First, he tightened the Smithsonian's grip on a key parcel of land that had most recently been used for parking and storage. Then he moved forward with yet another proposal to create a center for African, Near Eastern, and Asian culture with ample room for international activities such as the Smithsonian Institution Traveling Exhibition Service and its Office of International Relations. The complex would, said Ripley, form a "Quadrangle in the collegial sense."[6] It would have global reach as a theater for international activities and a university open to the world. A sudden flurry of brick-and-mortar projects to enliven these spaces would fix his own forceful and, he thought, enduring stamp on the institution he had been leading.

As the Quadrangle idea was taking shape in Ripley's mind, with conditional congressional approval in the late 1970s, Dr. Arthur Sackler stepped onto the playing field. The son of a New York entrepreneur wiped out by the Depression, Sackler worked as a delivery boy to get through medical school. Later he made a fortune from psychiatry, pharmaceuticals, and medical magazine publishing. As his coffers swelled, so did his interest in art as a fundamental expression of human creativity. In New York, starting in the mid-1940s, he insatiably bought not just individual pieces but entire collections. Along the way, convinced that Asian and Near Eastern art was particularly underappreciated and undervalued, he acquired thousands of works from those lands. An eventual consequence was a complex and difficult relationship with New York's Metropolitan Museum of Art, where he underwrote a new wing to house the Temple of Dendur. He also generously supported Asian art facilities at Harvard, Clark University, and elsewhere at home and abroad.

In 1979, having heard only vaguely of Sackler, who had amassed the largest private collection of Asian art in the United States, Ripley went to lunch at the National Gallery of Art with Sackler's lawyer, Michael Sonnenreich. The encounter was orchestrated by the National Gallery director, J. Carter Brown. Sonnenreich suggested a meeting with Sackler, which in turn led to the fashioning of a close friendship between Sackler, Ripley, and their wives. The warmth of this relationship stood in contrast to the litigious acrimony that had developed in New York. It smoothed the way toward Sackler's decision in 1982 to donate a thousand works from his Asian and Near Eastern art holdings, to be chosen by Smithsonian curators. What Sackler gave was worth $75 million in 1987. He also gave $4 million toward building the largely underground Arthur M. Sackler Gallery, which would embellish the southwest corner of the Quadrangle. Carter Brown claimed full credit for giving Sackler a steer toward the Smithsonian. But, Brown added, it was entirely Ripley who made the deal happen.

Asian art had been a major Smithsonian asset since 1906, when the industrialist Charles Lang Freer donated 2,250 objects from his magnificent collections. He also chipped in

$1 million for the building on the Mall to house them, which opened to the public in 1923. Freer's gift provided funds for an endowment for study and research, and for future acquisitions. The agreement also forbade the Freer to borrow works from elsewhere or allow art from its own collection to leave the premises. It was a restriction that, as Ripley observed, would enable the National Portrait Gallery to exhibit a Freer-owned object only if the Smithsonian truck making the delivery had a slowly unrolling ball of twine onboard to maintain the link. But with the Sackler Gallery alongside, equipped to manage a full range of conventional museum practices, the combined strength of the two galleries would establish them as world class in the Asian art field.

Arthur Sackler welcomed Ripley's sweeping approach, expecting that his gift would speed the way for Washington to become the nation's cultural capital and, he wrote, a beacon for

> millions of Americans, who annually make pilgrimages to our capital, usually with their families, to observe the extent to which we, as a people, are organically linked to other peoples, both in time and space. It is my hope that in presenting the manifestations of the cultures of the Pacific Basin, the Asiatic mainland, and the Middle East, will serve the function of building bridges of understanding and mutual respect between peoples of different backgrounds regardless of faith, racial origin of political ideology. It is an imperative of our times to recognize that all the components of culture — art, science, and the humanities — provide the most natural as well as the most fundamental spiritual, emotional, and intellectual bridges of communication between peoples.[7]

New Washington Homes for Art

A new opportunity to display African art was also emerging. This was thanks to a notable achievement on the part of a retired American diplomat, Warren Robbins. While posted as a cultural attaché in Europe during the 1950s, Robbins had developed a taste for African art and begun to build a collection. After he retired, he found a home for his own holdings and other donated works: the former Capitol Hill residence of the African American abolitionist Frederick Douglass. In 1964, his Museum of African Art opened there and enjoyed steady growth in activity and expansion into adjacent buildings.

Robbins was not a rich man enjoying the privileges of a Freer or a Sackler. But his more modestly scaled research led Robbins to feel that African art "represented one of humankind's great creative traditions." He saw that "if the general public—beyond the world of specialists and art lovers—could be made aware of that greatness, it might help break down the walls of prejudice that often separate black and white people."[8] The museum's success, fueled by a steady stream of financial support from large private foundations, individual philanthropists, and the newly created National Endowment for the Humanities, led to a need for additional space and a professional staff. Congress, with a major assist from the powerful senator Hubert Humphrey, had also voted to expand Robbins's museum. The museum merged into the Smithsonian in 1979.

The combination of these events, Ripley wrote,

> helped to trigger the project which had been gestating in my mind for years since the late 1970s, namely to create a Quad-

rangle of space, underground, adjacent to the three classic buildings of the Smithsonian—the original Castle, the adjacent Arts and Industries Building, and the Freer Gallery —forming a square, facing out to the south along Independence Avenue.[9]

Putting the Sackler and the African art museums underground would deflect opposition from Congress, and from the National Capital Planning Commission, to cluttering the crowded Mall with yet more large and expensive buildings. Digging down sixty feet would create ample space on three levels for both museums' galleries and exhibitions and for several of the Smithsonian's international activities. Under the terms of the Freer bequest, moreover, that museum had to remain a freestanding structure with no blending of its collection. So there was almost no option other than to dig down if the Freer and Sackler were to be near each other.

On the surface, small, elegant granite pavilions, alike but not twins, would mark the entryway into each museum, providing visitors with a "grand vestibule to prepare for their museum entry," as the Smithsonian historic preservation specialist Amy Ballard would describe it.[10] A small circular kiosk would signal the doorway to the International Center and an adjacent array of meeting rooms. A new public garden, featuring Islamic, Asian, and British Victorian elements, would handsomely cap the underground complex.

Ripley had reckoned that a woman who made conspicuously generous donations to garden projects, Enid A. Haupt, an Annenberg of the Philadelphia publishing family and a notoriously hard taskmaster, might take an interest in this new complex. Ripley commissioned sketches for a Zen garden within the Quadrangle, a "small, jewel-like spot for contemplation." Enid Haupt appeared one muddy March afternoon to inspect the site, causing Smithsonian faces to fall when she said no to the Zen garden and peppered the assembled staff with tough questions about details. Then, she added, her preference was to pay for the whole thing. And so she did, becoming a $4 million donor to the handsome rooftop landscape, completed in 1987, that remains known as the Enid A. Haupt Garden. An endowment came with the gift.

In contrast to other structures and pathways lined up between broad avenues along the Mall, the Haupt Garden is a calm space more suitable for meditation than for athletic pursuits. Near the Ripley Center entryway is the Moongate Garden, modeled after a Ming Dynasty garden at the Temple of Heaven in Beijing. Near the entryway into the African art museum is the Fountain Garden, where running water defines the Islamic-style interplay of circular and square elements. Victorian-style outdoor furniture and a central parterre help define these spaces as also suitable for contemplation and the enjoyment of floral beds.

For the Quadrangle's complex design and construction task, Ripley had engaged the Japanese architect Junzo Yoshimura. When he fell ill, responsibility shifted to the classic Boston firm of Shepley, Bulfinch, Richardson, and Abbott. A principal there was a Frenchman, Jean-Paul Carlhan, who had studied at the École des Beaux Arts in Paris and at Harvard. He became the project's point man to conduct what turned out to be a nine-year design, engineering, and construction charrette fraught with hazards. Extending well below the water table, the structure had to be made as watertight as a submarine. Specially designed polyester-wrapped steel rods called tiebacks were carefully installed to hold retaining walls in place. The greatest care could not prevent the entire Smithsonian Castle, close by and built of fragile sandstone, from sinking an inch and a half at one critical moment. One engineer feared that the whole Castle might collapse into the excavation before stabilizing measures were completed.

Here was yet another Houdini-like Ripley performance, featuring the drama of the courting of Dr. Sackler and of Enid Haupt, construction hazards, financial woes, and an eventual success marked by the triumphal 1987 opening of the Arthur M. Sackler Gallery. Ripley took the lead in raising the balance of the funds required, matching from private sources and foreign governments what had already been chipped in by a Ripley-charmed US Congress. A penniless idea hatched in Ripley's head had become a $73.2 million megaproject, leaving planners facing the challenge of making what became known as the Ripley Center reflect the Smithsonian's determination to be global in scope.

A Beachhead in New York

Soon after Ripley took charge, a way presented itself to plant a Smithsonian footprint in New York City by saving the Cooper Union Museum for the Arts of Decoration. This was an admired but small and needy old place on Cooper Square in lower Manhattan with important holdings, especially of textiles and wallpaper. The nation's only museum devoted exclusively to the decorative arts and design, the Cooper Union Museum was founded in 1896 by three Hewitt sisters, granddaughters of the philanthropist Peter Cooper, as a division of the Cooper Union for the Advancement of Science and

Art. Under the direction of the Hewitt sisters, the museum amassed its collection, which rivals that of the Musée des Arts Décoratifs in Paris in size and significance. For many years a devoted staff working with a tiny budget strove to keep the museum afloat in the face of stiff competition for funds from other branches of the Cooper Union. Push came to shove in June 1963, when, for want of sufficient income, the museum's board without prior warning announced plans to relocate the collections, and abruptly shuttered the doors.

The move prompted outcries of shock and dismay from cognoscenti. Henry F. du Pont of the chemical corporation family, who had founded the Winterthur Museum in Delaware, formed the Committee to Save the Cooper Union Museum, which began a spirited search for a savior. But he was not able to identify an angel anywhere in New York, not even at the mighty Metropolitan Museum of Art. It was interested only in cherry-picking from the Cooper Union collections and thus decreasing their value for researchers. Du Pont pinned his remaining hope—and perhaps the last recourse —on the Smithsonian. "Out of all the efforts that our Committee has pursued," he wrote, "the Smithsonian Institution has emerged as the single promising, truly interested, and sufficiently strong recipient of the Museum and its future development."[11]

In Ripley, du Pont found an eager prospective partner, who, from his childhood days in New York, recalled the Cooper Union Museum as "one of the principal ornaments in New York's cultural scene."[12] In a letter to the Cooper Union board chair, Arthur A. Houghton, Jr., Ripley professed the Smithsonian's "real and moral obligation" to try to help if no New York–based sponsor could be found.[13]After lengthy rounds of discussions and negotiations in the mid-1960s, Ripley and his regents agreed to take over the museum. Further digging and arm-twisting, with the crockery already rattling, resulted in a fateful decision by Andrew Carnegie's granddaughter Mrs. Carnegie Miller and the Carnegie Corporation. Made in 1967, the decision was to hand over to the Smithsonian the landmark, sixty-four-room Andrew Carnegie Mansion, on New York's "Museum Row" at Fifth Avenue and 91st Street, and retitle this new home the Cooper–Hewitt Museum of Design.

Now called Cooper Hewitt, Smithsonian Design Museum, it was the Institution's first museum venture beyond Washington. Ripley's old New York connections helped make the complex tour de force a reality. He felt comfortable dealing with those people and their lawyers. The renovated building opened to the public in October 1976 and closed again in 2008 for a six-year, $91 million upgrade. Reopened in 2014, the mansion now houses an intriguing mix of old wood paneling and space-age displays of great interest to children accustomed to clicking things around on video screens. Here, with digital access to collections and other techno-wonders, you can, for example, design your own wallpaper.

The Elusive Museum of Man

Intellectually, little challenged Ripley more than creating a national museum of man to rival existing anthropological museums in Paris and Mexico City. It would, Ripley wrote, boldly encompass "a summing up of the American experience, a synthesis of all that we have learned, the interactions of man on this part of the planet, the interface between ourselves and our environment."[14] It would respond to the challenge to anthropology that Claude Lévi-Strauss had issued at the 1965 convocation marking James Smithson's bicentennial year. Long-standing barriers between natural scientists on one wing and anthropologists on the other would be swept aside. As Ripley saw it, the schism occupied fragile ground:

> Objects which represented the culture of the primitive races of man were the specialty of the anthropologist, whose discipline, anthropology, rested on the uncomfortable assumption that the study of early man was somehow akin to biology. Anthropologists were not supposed to be interested in the Greeks or the Bible, but rather to concern themselves with Red Indians, noble savages, and, of course, Stone Age man. Perhaps, although this was dangerous ground, they might even be concerned with missing links?[15]

In the 1877 Musée de l'Homme in Paris, Ripley continued, one could find "exquisite records of extinct cultures." But, he added, "it is sad that no decorative or folk art of Western man is included after Neolithic times."[16] Mexico's magnificent National Museum of Anthropology represented a model for the Smithsonian to build on. Many existing Smithsonian units were already well positioned to become parts of the larger whole: the Office of Anthropology within the National Museum of Natural History, the Center for the Study of Man to promote interdisciplinary cultural and anthropological research, the very successful Folklife Festival, the National Anthropological Film Center, and the Office of American Studies. Artful direction might somehow get them all under the same roof, said Ripley in *Smithsonian Year 1967*, and in an excellent position to create a "modern Museum of Man" within which "all cultures and all humans should be accorded equal dignity and respect, and for this they deserve a museum of their own."[17]

Starting in the late 1960s, Ripley convened many gatherings and several committees to discuss how to move toward the establishment of a new national museum of man and requested input from many of his own colleagues. Some took a budget approach. Others designed organization charts. Frank Taylor, director of the US National Museum, posited a straightforward "Museum of Man and the Environment." Ripley himself wondered how such an austere subject could "convey a sense of fun."[18] He wrote several concept papers featuring the need for his version of the museum to address questions of food supply and demand and human population growth. The anthropologists squabbled over control issues, expressing concern about possible subordination to natural history scholars.

In 1969, Ripley had taken steps to "save Congress from themselves" by proposing legislation guaranteeing that the Smithsonian be awarded title to the prospective site of the national museum of man to be built on the last large building site on the Mall, the quadrilateral plot between 3rd and 4th Streets east of the National Air and Space Museum, along the Independence Avenue side where the National Museum of the American Indian now stands. "We wished to nail it down for future generations so that there would not be a sudden interruption in some orderly development of museum and public exhibit facilities on the Mall," he said, and in order to avoid the ever-present danger of someone championing the placement on the site of a memorial to a person or an event—or "pre-empt the site for congressional purposes."[19]

Meeting on November 5, 1969, the Smithsonian's regents endorsed the presentation of legislation authorizing the construction of a 350,000-square-foot building for the new mu-

seum at no cost to the Smithsonian. This building would enable the Smithsonian to remove "the sciences of man from
the Museum of Natural History," the bill stated, "and for the
first time put in a single worldwide context all studies and
exhibits of cultures and peoples from the earliest time to the
present."[20] Soon after, the bill was introduced in the House of
Representatives.

But there the project remained stalemated, a victim of
federal budget shortfalls and other hindrances to achieving a
federal appropriation. The National Park Service, which con-
trols the use of land on the Mall, continued to wonder why
the Smithsonian needed yet another museum building. Many
leaders on the Hill, especially the influential Rhode Island
senator Claiborne Pell, stood foursquare against building any
more marble palaces along the Mall. In a 1974 memorandum
to his regents, even Ripley himself confessed that "I rather
agree with him that probably we have done enough building
and construction for the time being."[21]

Ripley's own repeated efforts to convince his Smithsonian
colleagues of the project's paramount importance provoked
"many confused reactions," said David Challinor, the Smithsonian's assistant secretary for science and research, in a candid memorandum to Ripley.[22] The record, accumulated over
many years of staff debate, reveals several plaintive references
to the dormant idea. In the 1972 issue of *Smithsonian Year*,
Ripley urged deeper thought about "the problems of repre-
senting man in his environment, perhaps to be encompassed
in a Museum of Man."[23] He returned to the fray, calling in
the publication's 1974 issue for the creation of a "Museum of
the Family of Man." For the benefit of balky congressional
leaders, he put a new US spin on the concept, stating that the

new museum could "create a summing up of the American experience, a synthesis of all that we have learned." It would, he continued,

> include certain demonstrable American themes, including the history of the United States folk, who had come here, when and how, and how this has changed the land and sea and air, its past and present face . . . an informed projection of our evolution, both physically and culturally, into the future, our own Brave New World.[24]

None of this talk aroused a reaction from the Hill, and the designated site remained vacant for close to twenty years after Ripley's Smithsonian reign ended in 1984. Debate about the fate of the building site, which sputtered, finally ended in 1989, when Congress scrapped the museum of man idea and, at the behest of the Hawaii senator Dan Inouye, passed legislation authorizing the building of the National Museum of the American Indian (NMAI) on the designated site. The $219 million structure opened in 2004 with, some felt, an opportunity to take over Native American–related anthropology and ethnology functions that might have found their way to a museum of man with its global vision. But no staff member ever moved to NMAI from the Natural History Museum, which still maintains a full-fledged anthropology department.

It had been a rare defeat for Ripley. He had put up a less than fully convincing case for one of his most cherished dreams, thinking of his museum of man as doing much to define the entire institution. But his description left even David Challinor and others among his most loyal staff people confused about what he really wanted. He had floated the project without following his usual practice of recruiting enthusiastic cohorts on and off the Hill. There was no White House champion for it, no power broker eager to push it forward.

Most important, as the historian William Walker chronicles in minute detail, the idea ran counter to what had become the general flow of Smithsonian and Capitol Hill thinking about museums. The consensus now favored culturally specific projects over those loftily expressing cultural pluralism. Much as Ripley would favor those broadly probing humankind's "questing spirit from humanity's earliest days to the present," Walker concluded, Congress had come to prefer promoting the more specific talents of Native Americans or black Americans or aviators.[25] After all the huffing and puffing, what today remains of the idea is a modest, seldom-polished brass plaque, subordinating the "Museum of Man" name, at the teeming Constitution Avenue entryway to what is universally known as the National Museum of Natural History.

Air and Space Flies High

As the 1970s began, pressure mounted to celebrate the US Bicentennial by opening the National Air and Space Museum on the Mall. The concept for such a building had been in place since 1946, when Congress declared what was then called the National Air Museum to be a Smithsonian bureau. Since 1958, space for this museum had been reserved on the Mall, on the stretch between the Arts and Industries Building and the Capitol. In 1966, Congress had authorized up to $50 million for the project and added the word "space." But initial construction bids came in at $65 million or more, and in the tight budget climate of the Vietnam War years it seemed unlikely that Congress would appropriate that much. Even after the architect, Gyo Obata, came up with a simplified and lower-budget design, it took mighty persuasion on the part of Senator Barry Goldwater to move the project along.

In 1970, Goldwater, himself a World War II aviator, gave a well-researched speech in which he bitterly complained that not one cent had been spent on building the museum, its proposed location on the Mall was threatened, and it seemed far down on a Smithsonian priority list on which arts, humanities, public awareness projects, and "showy buildings" seemed to rank far higher. All he was seeking was a better balance, Goldwater said, and "a decent home for the national center where the world's greatest collection of aircraft and space objects can be shown."[26] The museum's director at the time, S. Paul Johnston, complained that he reported to the Smithsonian's assistant secretary for history and art, Charles Blitzer, whose prior academic expertise was in Britain's political history during the eighteenth century.

In 1971, the former astronaut Mike Collins was appointed to succeed Johnston, who retired after a frustrating five years of service. With Ripley's help and boundless enthusiasm, Collins brought around the incoming president, Richard Nixon, and key congressional leaders to wrestle the project through Congress. It was a cliffhanger, but approval was obtained. Construction at last began in 1972, and what was to become the most visited of all Smithsonian museums and, for more than two decades, the busiest museum in the world, opened in time for the July 4, 1976, Bicentennial ceremonies and scored 3 million visitors during its first three months. Ripley, not a huge fan of the project and overlooking its immense popularity, stressed its importance as an educational asset for young people.

For all the setbacks, most of Ripley's brick-and-mortar initiatives, on the Mall and beyond, have survived and prospered, making the Smithsonian look and feel ever more like the university of his dreams. But he could not have done all that he did without stirring up some significant dust of his own.

CHAPTER NINE

Waves of Complaints

Washington thrives on scandal, and not even the agile Mr. Ripley could entirely escape it. Three anti-Ripley outbreaks made headlines during the late 1960s and early 1970s. Attacks on his management capabilities, many stemming from irresponsible muckraking press coverage, resulted in an unprecedented round of congressional hearings.

Staff anthropologists and others hurled strident complaints against members of Ripley's carefully selected inner core of lieutenants, and warfare ensued. At the height of Vietnam War anxieties, scientists and the media voiced vociferous concern about broadly aired if exaggerated suspicions that Smithsonian scientists in the Pacific theater and in Amazonia were semisecretly conducting germ warfare research for the US military. Such was Ripley's skill that both he and the Smithsonian emerged better off for having endured the sharp questioning. But it was a trying time for Ripley as well as one replete with accomplishment.

In the summer of 1969, the US House of Representatives' Subcommittee on Library and Memorials, which had jurisdiction over the Smithsonian's federal funding, held hearings to review its management. These hearings, the first the venerable Smithsonian had been subjected to in a hundred years, were held over a seven-day period for the purpose of examining how the institution was spending its allocation of federal resources, then amounting to about $35 million a year, as well as some $15 million a year in grants and revenues from the private sector.

The outcome of the hearings was twofold, the subcommittee said. It found no evidence of mishandling of public funds, but requested more detailed reporting on the use of private funds. Ripley, whose testimony had won over the subcommittee members and staff, expressed delight that the hearings had been so informative. Congress member Frank Thompson, chair of the subcommittee, added that the hearings were "long overdue" and that he was very pleased about the outcome. He praised Ripley and "all your splendid people" for having on short notice "prepared carefully and very well done testimony." Congress member John Brademas, a subcommittee member who later became president of New York University, said that after posing some tough questions he came away "immensely impressed," adding that "the Smithsonian and the country are terribly fortunate to have leading that great institution a man of the imagination and capacity of Dr. Ripley."[1]

Merchant Mariner Sounds Off

Many of the accusations leading to the hearings stemmed from a self-appointed watchdog named Robert H. Simmons, who sometime in his adulthood became Robert Hilton Simmons. He was a man of many small parts. Born on Cape Cod, Massachusetts, the son of a telephone company worker, Simmons served during World War II aboard transport vessels, then earned poor grades studying Chinese art at the University of California in Berkeley. Later he followed his brother, a third mate for the Hawaiian-American Line, into service as a merchant mariner. As an officer aboard the luxury ocean liner *President Wilson*, Robert Simmons made frequent shipboard runs to the Pacific and acquired a motley collection of Chinese art—thirty-three pieces, which in 1948 were said to have been worth $15,000. In Shanghai he hoisted aboard the ship an old Chinese funeral urn that he had bought for $75 and later sold for $350.

After twenty years at sea Simmons settled in Washington, working as a naval intelligence analyst and adding to his collection an eclectic assortment of objects, including a number of pieces of kitsch that had belonged to J. Edgar Hoover, director of the FBI. Working as a freelance writer in the 1960s and '70s, Simmons became what the *Washington Post* later called "kind of a gadfly on the local art scene" and a founding board member of Warren Robbins's National Museum of African Art.[2] During the 1960s, he organized several exhibitions for that fledgling institution and continued to collect an odd mixture of art.

Early on, Simmons also became a frequent writer of letters to the editor, prominent citizens, and others. As a teenage merchant mariner during World War II, he honed his skills at this craft by sending unsolicited dispatches back home. Publishing them was what the editors of his hometown newspaper on the Cape, the *Falmouth Enterprise*, called an "occasional privilege" for their "humor and brightly turned phrase."[3] The drumbeat continued after his move to Washington. In 1973, his literary career may have peaked when the *Washington Post* published a letter of his in which, echoing Gilbert and Sullivan, he complained that the capital was overpopulated with lawyers. "Can there," he asked, "be any condition more dangerous to a genuine democracy than a government run by and having the character of lawyers?"[4]

As time passed, Simmons came to rely less on his own pen than on tipping off powerful commentators and congressional staffers on the Hill about what he felt were brewing scandals within Washington's slender cultural community. He particularly leveled broadsides at the Smithsonian and directly at Ripley. The muckraking journalist Jack Anderson, editor-author of the "Washington Merry-Go-Round" column, was a favored recipient. Several prominent *Washington Post* and *Washington Star* writers were also frequent beneficiaries of these "news tips," as was the ace investigative reporter Clark Mollenhoff of the *Des Moines Register.* For years, peaking in 1969, Simmons also directed a barrage of anti-Smithsonian alerts at influential elected officials, including Senators J. William Fulbright and Clifton Anderson, both of whom were serving as Smithsonian regents at the height of the storm in the late 1960s. Not even Warren Burger, chief justice of the Supreme Court, head of the Smithsonian's Board of Regents, and Dillon Ripley's boss, was spared the barrage of Simmons's allegations about Ripley's performance.

During the summer and fall of 1969, Simmons's campaign of harassment against Ripley and the Smithsonian reached full throttle. That autumn, Fulbright received four letters from Simmons. One hinted at conflict-of-interest and tax issues relating to the acquisition of the Hirshhorn collection. Simmons also raised questions about the sale of a Smithsonian-owned painting at an auction in London. Finally, in a letter dated November 26, 1969, Simmons promised Fulbright that he would continue his research on the Institution, which "deserves to be something better than the stronghold of a clique of gangsters."[5] Fulbright sent copies of these letters to Ripley, who told Fulbright, in an undated letter addressed to "Dear Bill," that "in view of the contentiousness and vagueness of his questions," it would be better not to reply.[6]

That fall, writing directly to the chief justice, Simmons unleashed a further barrage of rambling anti-Ripley accusations and recommendations. Convincing Congress to vote "an enormous sum" for the Hirshhorn Museum had left the Air and Space Museum shorthanded, he claimed, and Joseph Hirshhorn himself was "mixed up" in crooked tax write-off deals. "The fact is that he has not turned over a new leaf," he wrote Burger in a three-page, single-spaced rant dated October 10, 1969, "but that the Hirshhorn Museum deal was and is . . . a swindle in which, I believe, the American people have been victimized."[7] In one of several similar letters, Simmons explained to Burger that "the Congress was maneuvered into authorizing an enormous sum for the building and maintenance of the Hirshhorn Monument on the Mall." Several hundred historic guns had disappeared from the Museum of History and Technology with no explanation, he stated, and the matter had been "hushed up."[8]

"I may add that I have nothing personal whatever against Dr. S. Dillon Ripley," Simmons said in his October 7, 1969, letter to the chief justice. "I have never met him—except for a few seconds in the Museum of Natural History in 1965 when I was selecting African works of art for inclusion in a book. He happened into the gallery and I expressed admiration for the new installation. He seems to have a pleasant personality, and has done apparently significant work in the field of ornithology."[9]

On October 13, 1969, Ripley wrote Burger to apologize for

his having been bothered by the "rather strange interest" that Simmons had taken in the Smithsonian and to promise a full statement in response.[10] On November 19, at the request of Senator Clinton Anderson, Ripley delivered a memorandum in which he refrained from commenting on the "multitude of peripheral issues, red herrings, and innuendoes" included in the Simmons fusillade.[11] It was, Ripley added, "something of a relief" to be addressing Jack Anderson's "extraordinarily intemperate" and "patently false" allegations "openly and directly" rather than trying to react to "vague rumors" about them.[12]

In his memorandum Ripley argued that the Smithsonian had faithfully followed standard museum practices when engaged in the admittedly delicate matter of selling artworks from its collections. He especially commented on the sale, for $120,000, of a work by the Italian artist Francesco Guardi that was of limited interest to the National Collection of Fine Arts, a specialist in American art. He had acted in the national interest when, working with White House staff advisers and directly with President and Mrs. Lyndon Johnson, he had secured by a 1967 act of Congress the splendid Hirshhorn collection and funds to place it in a new building on the Mall. One issue was the valuation of the works, about which Simmons had fulminated in the belief that Hirshhorn was getting an illegal tax break in return for his gift. He had it "on good authority," Simmons had argued, that IRS reevaluations were $10 million to $20 million too high.[13] This was none of the Smithsonian's business, Ripley countered. What was important for the Institution was the collection's artistic merit.

Roger Stevens, the powerful entrepreneur who had advised many occupants of the White House on cultural matters, also

argued strongly in Ripley's defense on the Hirshhorn question. "As Assistant to the President on the arts at that time,"
he wrote in a May 22, 1970, letter to the *New York Times*, "it
was my job to try to improve the government's position in
the arts." He had worked closely on the proposed Hirshhorn
accession, and it was he who proposed the White House luncheon that had clinched the deal. Then Ripley took over the
helm and, Stevens continued, it was "thanks to his zeal and
persuasiveness that the negotiations were concluded." Directly
challenging one of the Jack Anderson attacks, said Stevens,
"the article contained innuendoes that there were tax gim-
micks involved."

> Obviously, anyone making gifts to art museums is entitled
> to deductions of the fair market value of his gift. Since Mr.
> Hirshhorn started his collection many years ago, it is only
> reasonable to assume that its value would be far in excess of
> its actual cost since it is a well-known fact that paintings and
> sculpture have increased tremendously in value over the past
> several decades. In any case, the Internal Revenue Service can
> be expected to very carefully examine a gift of this magnitude,
> and it is well able to take care of itself. In addition, the value
> of this gift is so great that Mr. Hirshhorn could not possibly
> have enough income to make a tax deduction the reason for
> making the gift."[14]

In 1972, according to the *Washington Post*, Simmons was
working on a book about federal art programs and more specif-
ically about the Smithsonian and Ripley's alleged managerial
shortcomings. Though no Simmons book was ever published,
Jack Anderson wrote that it was "actually a biting, personal
expose of Ripley himself and his management of Smithsonian
funds."[15] In a 1970 column, Anderson claimed that Ripley

had used $2,800 in government funds in partial payment for chartering a yacht on the Aegean Sea to visit archaeological sites and search for the rarely seen Audouin's gull. For two weeks during the summer of 1969, wrote Anderson, Ripley "sailed the wine-dark seas around the isles of Greece. . . . He quaffed fine drink, lolled on beaches, sampled succulent Palaiokastritsa lobsters and viewed antiquities, all at public expense."[16] Challenged, Ripley's staff stated that private donors had approved and financed the expedition, during which not only the gull, but another rare bird, the Eleanora's falcon, was spotted. Ripley said that looking for the birds was an afterthought, as had been fully explained to the private donors, to the trip's principal purpose: a symposium in the Mediterranean on Bronze Age cultures that he and Mary Ripley helped organize and attended.

There were other allegations of financial mismanagement, as well as a burst of criticism from within the Institution. A notoriously cranky anthropologist named Clifford Evans had, shortly before Ripley's 1964 arrival at the Smithsonian, taken the leadership in forming a "Senate of Scientists" to facilitate communications between them and top-level administrative bureaucrats and to try to overrule whatever they disliked. Ripley and Evans quickly established a keen distaste for each other. "When Ripley and I meet anywhere it's like two unfriendly tigers in a cage," said Evans. "He practically ignores me and I practically ignore him." Evans felt that he was fighting for "principles," of unstated varieties, against a funds-juggling Ripley surrounded by "flunkies and his right-hand men and all his wild-haired programs. . . . Ripley had no use for us because we questioned his judgment."[17] Though most of the Institution's top officials and scientists loved working for

Ripley and were loyal to their "Sun King," Evans's reactions, needling from the media, and Simmons's random salvos were enough to set off a reaction and calls for hearings on the Hill.

Clean Bill from the Hill

Despite the clean bill of health from the Thompson hearings, anti-Ripley accusations persisted through the 1970s, and there were periodic audits by the federal government's General Accounting Office. Jack Anderson kept up the chatter, firing a new blast in 1974 about Ripley family travel at government expense. In 1977, reported the *Washington Star*, Ripley was again "under the gun" and "trying to stay out of range of potshots from Capitol Hill and some members of the media."[18] But the wily Ripley managed to succeed in consistently countering "a steady barrage of press stories implying but never nailing down skullduggery." Often he was conveniently "on travel" when summoned by the Hill. He even disarmed Jack Anderson, who wrote, "In three long talks with us, Ripley ably defended his long absences from the Smithsonian. His critics concede that his innovative management has transformed Washington's famous Mall and its museums into an exciting center for art, music, and festivals."[19]

The regents remained loyal during what was by any reckoning a hard time for the Institution and for Ripley personally. Dealing with critics is "never an easy job," said one of them, Thomas J. Watson, Jr., of the family that ran IBM. But his own experience told him, he said in an August 26, 1970, letter to Ripley, that "the only way to handle this kind of criticism is to readily admit errors where they exist." If the implication was that Ripley had indeed made some mistakes, Watson kept this to himself and offered consoling thoughts: "I know the past few months have been trying ones for you; and it has probably been difficult to maintain a balanced outlook. You have done a remarkable job of bringing a new sense of importance and direction to the Smithsonian and, as is always the case with change, there are those who will take issue with it."[20]

Pacific Troubles

While fighting off these challenges in the late 1960s, Ripley also found himself, to his surprise, amid another huge "foo-faw," as the *Smithsonian* magazine's Ed Thompson would have called it, about Pacific Ocean bird research that Smithsonian scientists had been conducting semisecretly under what was initially a $208,000 contract to the Army Chemical Center in Fort Detrick, Maryland, which had first been signed on October 9, 1962, pre-Ripley, and was renewed each year up to 1970. As part of what it called Operation Starbright, the military called on the Smithsonian to supply researchers to embark on fifteen-day naval cruises to remote, uninhabited islands in the vast, largely unexplored central Pacific region and record all visible animal life. A large number of seabirds would be captured, and blood samples would be collected. Most of them would be tagged in the hope of future recovery, as part of an effort to obtain new information about their migratory routes. Some would be brought back alive. Oceanographic data would also be collected from a 50,000-square-mile, almost uninhabited portion of the central Pacific, seven hundred miles south of Hawaii, as a principal feature of what became known as the Pacific Ocean Biological Survey Program or POBS. During the life of the giant project, no fewer than 1,800,000 birds would be banded. The researchers would record some 150,000 bird observations and conduct full-fledged biological surveys on several islands.

Within the Smithsonian, scientists and others initially greeted these arrangements with gratitude and enthusiasm. The project would add new chapters to a 150-year history of nonclassified cooperation between the Institution and the military in a quest for ways to help fulfill the Smithsonian's mandate "for the increase and diffusion of knowledge." Scarce funds would support the POBS work, supplying ample opportunities for the researchers to establish baseline information about an immense area that had rarely been studied by scientists. Starving ornithologists gleefully signed up. Philip Humphrey, POBS project director and chair of the Smithsonian's Department of Vertebrate Zoology, waxed eloquent about the opportunity the military had provided. As he put it:

> Perhaps the most important practical accomplishment of the Smithsonian survey will be the delineation of the environment over a relatively short period of time. This will provide a baseline of comparison for biologists concerned, 10 or 20 years from now, with measuring the effects of man-made modifications of the environment on natural populations of organisms. The need for such a baseline is most urgent today, when man, in his struggle to advance himself, is changing the face of the earth at an appallingly rapid rate, and is subjecting the total environment—water, atmosphere, and living tissues—to physical and chemical influences which need to be measured now and in the future. For unless these fundamental changes in his environment are properly assessed, man himself, through ignorance, may fall victim to his own progress.[21]

Despite the euphoria, the project's field scientists began to emit little cries of alarm as they launched their studies. They wondered why they were compelled to get security clearances, why they were told to destroy some of their documents, why some of their documents became classified as secret, why they were asked to be "careful" about how they described their work to outsiders. They were instructed to use general words such as "ecology" and "military" and to avoid specifying the destination of live-bird shipments. In no sense were they living a lie, wrote the journalist Ted Gup. Rather, the Smithsonian was issuing "a selective rendering of the truth."[22] Ripley's Office of Strategic Services background aroused suspicions.

These apprehensions were creeping out at a time during the Vietnam War era when military units were studying many fanciful ways to wage war. "Military exotica flourished: mind control through drugs, porpoises as animate torpedoes, new concoctions of chemical and biological weapons, " Gup continued. "It was a macabre time of Strangelovean fantasies when even one of God's gentlest creatures, a gull, could be considered for a doomsday assignment." No one accused the Smithsonian of directly participating in biological weapons testing. Still, wrote the Australian historian Roy MacLeod in a 2001 article entitled "Strictly for the Birds," "the participation of Smithsonian staff in secret military-oriented research projects came as a shock to the national psyche."[23] It was not long before the media got into the game: a February 5, 1969, report by the NBC News correspondent Tom Pettit touched off a frenzy of speculation and a flurry of Smithsonian denials of participation in biological warfare research.

Initially, after the story broke, Ripley feigned ignorance.

"To me, as a bird man, this was a wonderful breakthrough because it was a source of funds," he said. "That's all I know about it."[24] But at levels below his, the Institution's public relations machine worked feverishly to clear its name from any sort of involvement in germ warfare research, and the subject gradually faded. The project was officially and quietly terminated in June 1970.

But the story did not end before Ripley had to endure yet another major tiff between him and the Senate of Scientists. The anthropologist Clifford Evans, during the period when he chaired that body, was also conducting Amazonian research and learned that birds from the Amazon were being shipped to Fort Detrick. With suspicions aroused that the Smithsonian was indeed involved in clandestine germ warfare research, Evans and several other scientists confronted Sidney Galler, then the assistant secretary for science, about "all sorts of secret hanky-panky." Eventually, they won a policy commitment that "no Smithsonian scientist shall ever be involved in any research or receive funds from any source that is or becomes secret." The establishment of the principle satisfied David Challinor, who succeeded Galler in 1971 and had smelled a POBS rat early on. "By God," Challinor said to Ted Gup, "it would be over my dead body if that thing were ever cranked up again."[25]

This was not Ripley's finest hour. His protestations of innocence did him little good: the issues raised were of such importance that, no matter how much or how little he knew, only he could credibly defend the Institution. The murky episode had, said Roy MacLeod, been one of "changing meanings and misgivings, of confusion between means and ends, of ambition and of conscience . . . combining elements of fact and speculation." The whole flap, he continued, revealed the Smithsonian as a

> benign if somewhat bifocal agency, caught off guard and finding itself, in the middle of the Vietnam War, in an uncomfortable relationship to military sponsorship. Before the 1960s, no one questioned the Smithsonian's patriotism or its place in the spectrum of government sponsored research. By the late 1960s, however, the public mood had shifted . . . and the Castle had not kept pace. The Pacific program was a perfect manifestation of the Institution's desire to be of service to government, coupled with an understandable keenness for government funds and facilities. But the Smithsonian enjoyed a special, almost unique position of public trust — exemplified by the public's affection for its museums, its zoo, and its Secretary, S. Dillon Ripley, a man of high scholarship and integrity, widely respected in the scientific community and Congress. It was this sense of public trust that, some argued, had been betrayed by what seemed like an unseemly cohabitation with interests that were then waging a chemical, if not also biological war in South East Asia.[26]

The bruised Smithsonian, having undergone what MacLeod called a problematic moment in its history, had learned a major lesson. It would emerge with a sounder policy on what kinds of research funds to accept. And Ripley would have another thirteen years to rub his Aladdin's lamp and work his customary magic on the fast-growing Institution.

CHAPTER TEN

Science and Conservation

For all that Ripley accomplished as the Smithsonian's cultural maestro, his somewhat separate life as a working scientist and nature conservationist also warrants respectful attention. Despite his many other obligations, Ripley made time to do his own scientific research, as often as possible slipping away to his musty lab at the National Museum of Natural History, where for many years he plugged away at ornithology projects. Somehow he managed to publish some three hundred scientific papers, many of them written on Smithsonian time, as well as coauthor with Sálim Ali the monumental *Handbook of the Birds of India and Pakistan*. He also wrote an impressive assortment of engaging speeches, annual report essays, and popular articles and books for lay readers.

The major effort by Ripley and Ali to assemble the handbook had dramatically reversed the prevailing division of responsibilities between developed-country biologists and local Third World counterparts. Ripley continued to enjoy doing the measuring and classifying grunt work that many research scientists viewed as drudgery. Ali took the broader view, according to Ripley, by introducing the more modern concepts of ecology to India.

Environmental setbacks had begun to awaken scientists to the need for action as well as research. As the planet became ever more beset by sloppy development, overharvesting of resources, and pollution, leaders in the natural sciences shifted toward a broader, more holistic agenda. Zoology gave way to ecology and the study of how many kinds of plants and animals got along and related to each other in worsening physical environments, and relatively pristine ones as well. Many biologists became global ecologists, who pioneered waves of new discoveries along evolutionary pathways previously explored by Charles Darwin Alexander von Humboldt and Alfred Russel Wallace, and later by the American Museum of Natural History's Ernst Mayr, Yale's Evelyn Hutchinson, Harvard's E. O. Wilson, Princeton's Robert MacArthur, and Thomas Lovejoy.

Nature conservation gained ground at midcentury, as more and more undescribed species were said to be headed for extinction before they had even been discovered or their potential value to human health and well-being assessed. Bookstores featured works like Barry Commoner's *The Closing Circle* (1971) and Rachel Carson's *Silent Spring* (1962). Preserving threatened habitats rich in biological diversity became a top conservation priority. Today, what became known as biodiversity remains a compelling global goal, though no longer as fashionable a concern as it was in the 1970s and 1980s, currently partially eclipsed by more recently heightened worries about climate change, sea level rise, and other water- and health-related issues. Finding no indication that foreign policy and foreign aid planners had "ever heard of ecology or would know how to talk to a systematic biologist," Ripley joined his friend and mentor Evelyn Hutchinson in charging sometimes-reluctant scientists with a "social duty to alert citizens to the suicidal consequences" of a human-generated assault on the planet. In his view conservation had become the "ultimate responsibility."[1]

As time passed, Ripley's name appeared ever more frequently on the short list of key personalities who guided and expanded the world conservation movement. He served as a high-ranking international advocate of conservation at the International Union for the Conservation of Nature and Natural Resources, the International Council for Bird Preservation, and the World Wildlife Fund, where for seven years starting in 1981 he chaired the US board. He was a senior officer of many other boards and commissions concerned with protecting the global environment. At international meetings and conferences, especially those taking place during his later years at the Smithsonian, he was able to address the global conservation agenda from these platforms, captivating audiences with urgent messages delivered in his distinctive voice with its plummy, British-accented overtones.

Saving Endangered Species

From time to time, Ripley was able to fasten widespread attention to the plight of a single charismatic species or a spot on the planet of particular significance. He did much to protect from overhunting the once plentiful Bengal tiger, which in 1969 he had predicted would be extinct in twenty years but which has experienced a modest comeback in India, with 2,226 individuals recently recorded. He worked with a fellow aviculturist, Sir Peter Scott, to prevent Hawaii's nene goose from going extinct. The unique environment of Ecuador's

Galapagos Islands and the Charles Darwin Research Station based there were lifelong concerns.

In a pungent speech he gave in 1983, Ripley summarized his views on international conservation. We are all in this together, he said, "within a common fragile envelope which we are busy plundering as we will, those of us who belong to developed nations just as surely as those of us who knowingly or unknowingly do the same in the less developed parts of the world." What is needed, he added, is a global "green army" to replace the current military, which has "nothing to offer except destruction," and work toward the topmost goals of "environmental health and the preservation of biological diversity." Unless we pull ourselves together, Ripley warned, we are all "doomed to live in a wasteland, not created by nature or by high technology such as nuclear attack, but rather by man's inadvertence and by human frailty."[2]

In 1981, in an interview at northern California's Point Reyes Bird Observatory (now called Point Blue), Ripley got more specific about how he would go about protecting endangered species. Particularly he meant the California condor, then down to its last few individuals. There was no doubt about the subject's importance, Ripley said, for endangered species served as "a kind of early warning system to changes in the planetary health that we hope to preserve." Care, attention, and rules were often insufficient, although a combination of public awareness and careful range management, as in the instance of the whooping crane, could sometimes arrest declines. Rather than embrace triage strategies to benefit the most robust of the endangered, Ripley felt that "every case has to be measured on its own merits." On his spectrum, habitat protection was often the top choice even if the measure failed to save individual species or subspecies.[3]

One of Ripley's classic campaigns, to save an Indian Ocean tortoise species, epitomizes his willingness to seek out anybody who might help avert a costly loss for biodiversity. Some 100,000 giant, 350-pound tortoises inhabited the group of Indian Ocean islands called Aldabra. Found nowhere else on earth, the Aldabra tortoise, ungainly cousin of the Galapagos tortoises, is "as big as a bathtub," said Ripley, "not an enormous bathtub, but a pretty good-sized bathtub that even I could have a bath in."[4] Aldabra, a chain of 92 islets 265 miles north of Madagascar, is the world's second-largest coral atoll. It covers almost 60 square miles and is the most remote part of the Seychelles, a British crown colony in recent times, 700 miles away from its capital, Mahe. Without freshwater or arable soil, Aldabra was in the 1960s populated by only a handful of research scientists and supporting staff members, and remains in almost pristine condition despite occasional visits by closely supervised cruise ships and dive boats. In addition to the resident tortoises, Aldabra hosts flamingos, ibises, and other seabirds as well as a tiny warbler and a flightless rail.

The atoll was flooded some 175,000 years ago. No plants or animals other than the tortoise survived. A more recent threat came from a nineteenth-century British woodcutting project that drew successful protests by British scientists, including Charles Darwin, and from the harvesting of tortoises and turtles for meat and shell. In 1964, Ripley saw a squib in the newspaper saying that the British had chosen Aldabra as a good site for a marine radar station and had approached the United States about the possibility of joint management and the construction of an airstrip. It seemed to him, said Ripley, that this "would be the end of the flora and fauna and uniqueness of the island."[5] He had read of earlier instances where Smithsonian secretaries had advised sitting presidents on environmental issues, and instructed Mrs. Gabriel, his secretary, to make an appointment with Defense Secretary Robert McNamara to discuss "a matter of considerable importance."[6]

McNamara "barely looked up from his papers" when Ripley walked into his office, but paid closer attention when Ripley said that the $35 million construction project would amount to pouring money down the drain. "This was his lingo even though perhaps I was glossing it a bit," said Ripley. He also noted that large soaring birds would get ingested in jet plane engines, causing damage that could kill aircrews. McNamara handed the issue over to his deputy Paul Nitze, a birder and, not surprisingly, a friend of Ripley's. Discussions also involving William Warner, Ripley's "righthand handyman," moved forward.[7] Help came from the prominent British biologist Julian Huxley and from Evelyn Hutchinson, who argued that the project would wipe out the tortoises and leave a permanent gap in our understanding of the natural world. After a year of deliberations, the idea was quashed—a rare instance of environmentalists trumping the military-industrial complex—and eventually Aldabra became a carefully protected UNESCO World Heritage Site.

"Thank God," said McNamara. "I've had these scientist fellows on my back for months."[8]

CHAPTER ELEVEN

Retiring the Crown

D uring the later part of his long tour of duty, Ripley remained fully engaged. He was ready to step down, but had hoped to stay on for an extra year in order to be in charge of the Quadrangle opening. It therefore came as a shock when the Smithsonian Board of Regents, led by Chief Justice Warren Burger, with whom Ripley did not get along, pushed him aside as his long run was coming to an end. Being sidelined at the key moment in the evolution of the Smithsonian's South Campus was, he said, his principal regret about retiring when told he had to.

Yanking Ripley away at that critical moment, many people felt, constituted insensitivity of the worst sort. In a *Hartford Courant* interview, the major garden donor Enid Haupt said she had angrily told Burger that it was a terrible mistake. "He said it had been 20 years; it was time for a new secretary. And I told him, you're wrong. Dillon was a genius, and he should have been allowed to stay on."[1] In 1985, Ronald Reagan awarded Ripley the Presidential Medal of Freedom, the nation's top federal decoration for a civilian. But not even this high honor could dispel the bad feeling among many Ripley loyalists.

The situation resembled the kind of dispassionate avoidance in which corporate officers specialize when discarding a fallen chief executive, letting the castaway leave a final board meeting without even a perfunctory expression of thanks for service. In the heavy air of unspoken bitterness that underlay the final days of his stewardship, Ripley voiced gallant sentiments in various Smithsonian publications, bravely saying in his 174th and last column in the magazine's "View from the Castle" page that his experience had been a "joyous one." He was eloquent in his final submission to the Institution's annual report, in which he called on the Smithsonian to be the bellwether for a nation badly in need of restoration:

> Across the Mall, even on calm days, gusts and eddies of breeze remind one that this is a vast, still, quite open space. The wind, when it comes unpredictably, blows hither and yon. Sometimes the flags round the Washington Monument stand straight out, their whipping sound rising to a continuous muted roar like rapids in a stream in spate. . . . Let us then summon those strange winds to our cause and make the view of the Mall one of hope, of keening winds blowing our flags straight and whipping shrill.[2]

As of that bittersweet moment, how might one best sum up Ripley's principal accomplishments on and off the Mall, around Washington, and around the world? The answer involves revisiting his record with regard to the Smithsonian's array of art and science museums. Beyond the Smithsonian, we have already examined Ripley's more personal role as a working scientist and as a leading advocate for the conservation of nature and the planet's priceless biodiversity.

The Cultural Record

For all the care Ripley took to bolster the Smithsonian's complex of museums, it is ironic that he was never able to win congressional support for the one he most wanted to create, a museum of man, to advance public understanding of human ecology. But he did add an unprecedented eight new museums (as well as seven research and storage facilities) to the Smithsonian's galaxy of bureaus and the quality and quantity of Smithsonian scholarship reached new heights.

Landing the Hirshhorn art collection was a triumph against long odds. So was the construction of Washington's first museum devoted to modern art, a controversial building but one of undeniable importance. The donation of the eight thousand objects in the Hirshhorn art collection lifted the Smithsonian into high-ranking prominence. The Arthur M. Sackler Gallery and the Freer, each with its own set of strengths, established the Smithsonian as a major force in the Asian art field. The arrival of the National Museum of African Art as a key component of the Quadrangle filled a conspicuous gap.

In 1968, the Old Patent Office Building in Washington flourished as the freshly renovated home of two museums featuring American artistic creativity. Along one side of the building, the National Portrait Gallery became what Ripley called a "uniquely original museum: a source of visual information about famous Americans."[3] Significantly, it had won a broadened mandate to include photographs among its holdings. In the same building, the National Portrait Gallery shares space with what, after several name changes, is now called the Smithsonian American Art Museum. That name, Ripley said, was "a rather grandiose handle for the eclectic, interesting, yet fragmentary group of *objets* that dustily reposed in Hall 10 of the Natural History Museum."[4] Ripley consolidated the Institution's art collections, haphazardly accumulated under five different secretaries He brought in a respected art historian, Joshua Taylor, as its director. Initial relations between the new directors chosen to lead these museums were not smooth, but they improved as each settled into a new chair.

With help from President Johnson and Jacqueline Kennedy, Ripley saved from demolition the Renwick Gallery, commissioning a renovation to establish it as a focal point for the decorative arts. With energetic leadership, it began to enjoy a new life as a cameo museum when it reopened in 1976 under the aegis of the National Museum of American Art. The Cooper–Hewitt acquisition further strengthened the Smithsonian's decorative arts holdings and opened a Smithsonian window in New York.

To support these changes and far more, the Institution's $200 million budget just for the 1980 fiscal year was equivalent to all of its spending from the outset in 1847 to the year of Ripley's arrival. A major use of those resources was to begin turning the Mall into "a park for people, a lawn of living celebrations."[5] The very successful Folklife Festival ranked high on Ripley's tally sheet, attracting hundreds of thousands of visitors a year to exhibit varieties of popular culture in ways that were new to traditional museums. The Anacostia Neighborhood Museum was innovative in its design and programs. In each instance these new institutions put into practice Ripley's concept of open education, pushing museums out onto the street and encouraging the public to feel more welcome inside as well. Ripley broke down many barriers, altering the world's general idea of what a museum was.

Sponsorship of the Woodrow Wilson Center for International Scholars gave Ripley new prestige if not power. *Smithsonian* magazine was an unexpected triumph. William Warner directed the Smithsonian's international activities with what

Ripley called "peripatetic éclat,"[6] helping UNESCO save Abu Simbel in Egypt, doling out increments of blocked local currencies to support US scientists' work overseas, and prompting international dialogue at the highest level by means of seminars and symposia.

Much progress was made on the transformation of the Smithsonian spaces into the university-like Quadrangle that Ripley struggled so hard to fashion as an appropriate environment for serious education and scholarship. For all his success over the short term, recent events would illustrate the fragility and ephemeral nature of this effort. For many years, visitors enjoyed the calm of the Enid A. Haupt Garden and the many uses of the subterranean spaces of the Quadrangle. Thanks to an ambitious master planning effort for the South Mall that was launched in the 2010s, the longevity of this complex would prematurely come under threat. The debate would be prolonged.

Few could argue against renovating the historic Smithsonian Castle, which had not had a major infrastructure refit in forty-four years and suffered damage from a freak earthquake that struck in 2001. Misuse as well as neglect dogged the Castle long after the Ripley years, with a succession of mutilations marring the grandeur of its Great Hall. The Arts and Industries Building adjacent to the Castle cried out for adaptive reuse. Initial planning also threatened major change to the South Mall structures and gardens, including the Haupt Garden. Here the grand scheme began running into opposition from some in the historic preservation and architecture communities.

At his peak during the Lyndon B. Johnson presidential years of the late 1960s, Ripley not only ran the Smithsonian but also served as chair of the top-drawer Federal Council of the Arts and Humanities and was a major voice at the Woodrow Wilson Center. Ripley outflanked even the National Gallery of Art's talented director, J. Carter Brown, and New York aspirants, to win the media's accolade as the nation's cultural czar. As the *Washington Post*'s architecture critic, Wolf Von Eckardt, described him, Ripley doubtless ranked as "one of culture's most dashing suitors" in Washington.[7] Comparisons with Andre Malraux, France's eminent and brainy culture minister under de Gaulle, were often made.

Getting It Done

So what were the forces within Ripley that somehow kept it all straight? How did he get all that science and conservation, education and policy done, especially during those twenty years when he had an immensely complicated and implacable institution to run? What were the hallmarks of his brand of leadership? There are no flat answers. But there are a few clues, and a lot has to do with self-assurance and style.

Ripley was a member of practically everything, at least a hundred organizations by one count. At dress-up events, his chest burst with decorations from many lands, and he wore his academic robes with pride. He was equally comfortable in shirtsleeves out on the street, manifesting his keen interest in diversity, pluralism, and civil rights. He had "nerve, charm, wit, and great intelligence," said his close associate Charles Blitzer, though it remained "a mystery how he imposed his will on such a large place."[8] Part of it was that when he was around, he was truly around. He restlessly wandered the Institution's corridors, knocking on unfamiliar doors to ask those he encountered what they were doing. "He visited us," said Sally Maran, an early employee of *Smithsonian* magazine, when I reached her by phone. "No other secretary ever did that."[9]

His ubiquity sometimes yielded unexpected benefits, as when Mary White, a staff assistant, spotted a tall, handsome man in the Smithsonian's Arts and Industries Building, standing alone before the famous airplane called the *Spirit of St. Louis*. She introduced herself, said Mr. Ripley was having lunch at his desk, and invited Charles Lindbergh up to the office to join him. "It was a long visit," said Ms. White.[10] Over the years the Castle brimmed with distinguished guests, from Pope John Paul II to Queen Elizabeth II and other British royals, to countless political leaders from many lands and the odd rock star. Frisbees and kites flew over the Mall in dense numbers at annual festivals. Medals were conferred frequently, often at the elaborate ceremonies that Ripley cherished. "It wasn't his fault that his blood was blue," said Paul Perrot, a loyal Ripley advocate who spent twelve Smithsonian years as assistant secretary for museum programs, during an interview. Ripley was not a snob.[11]

Ripley's livelier Smithsonian did much to pep Washington up and help refashion the town into the cultural center that he foresaw and promoted. He would have respected the downtown awakening that began during the early 2000s, when theater and music boomed in Washington, and new cafés and restaurants for diverse swarms of Millennials proliferated along 14th Street, scene of the most violent race riots of the 1960s. That said, the large-format Phillips Brooks appointment calendars on which he relied, cluttered with barely legible penciled-in notations and erasures, suggests little direct interest on his part in such places. He preferred clubs and was often found at the Metropolitan Club, Chevy Chase Club, or Cosmos Club in Washington or at the Century or the Knickerbocker in New York. A favorite was the Alibi, an eccentric downtown retreat that lacks a public telephone number or a visible street address, to which a carefully selected few members still gather on Fridays for lunch of indifferent quality but good companionship and conversation.

Ripley's social schedule was perpetually overloaded. Beyond the many large gatherings on the Mall, an example being the annual July Fourth celebration on the roof of the National Museum of American History, and the many ribbon cuttings and openings of exhibitions or new buildings or wings, there were frequent dinners or luncheons at the spacious Ripley residence on Embassy Row's Sheridan Circle. These were seated affairs, fourteen or sixteen people attending, often featuring fresh produce or flowers brought down from Litchfield and goods Mary Ripley herself had baked. The guests tended to be people of political importance, but family members and social friends were often squeezed in as well. To some of these people, Mary seemed aloof, imperious, a little stiff, and almost Edwardian in demeanor, perhaps a bit shy. Others, especially those who visited the Ripleys in Litchfield, where she was often surrounded by grandchildren and a succession of barely controllable dogs that she adored, found in her a warm heart and an adventuresome spirit.

There was about Ripley an air of New England hardheadedness and determination. According to Marc Pachter, who under and after Ripley occupied several key Smithsonian positions, "He never took no for an answer."[12] He was often willing to take a chance. If *Smithsonian* magazine had failed, the big gamble he took with it would probably have cost him his job. "If he thought something was a good idea," said his youngest daughter, Sylvia Addison, "he'd assume there was money for it somewhere. And if one route didn't work he would try something else."[13]

Ripley was a master at delegating while remaining softly in control. To this end, he assembled at the Smithsonian a kitchen cabinet of talented and trusted deputies. Ripley found Paul Perrot at the Corning Museum in upstate New York; after his twelve years overseeing the Smithsonian's museum programs, he finished his career as director of the elegant Virginia Museum of Fine Arts in Richmond. "Why he selected me was an undeniable mystery," Perrot said when we spoke. "He was so trusting. I had independence. It was challenging and quite wonderful."[14] He knew that if he found himself in trouble, said Perrot, Ripley would back him up. The political science professor Charles Blitzer was a ranking official of the American Council of Learned Societies before joining the Smithsonian, where, as assistant secretary for history and art, he often served as Ripley's alter ego and closest adviser. He recalled Ripley as a "master of indirection" who made a prospective colleague jump through many hoops before actually offering the job.[15] The Smithsonian's assistant secretary for science and research, David Challinor, a candid and highly trusted adviser, was an unabashed admirer who worked for Ripley for a quarter-century. The secretary, said Challinor, was seldom wrong.[16]

Much of Ripley's success as a multitasker came in large measure because of these and other talented people whom he brought in from far outside the entrenched bureaucracy and to whom he delegated large portions of responsibility. Some

chiefs of individual Smithsonian bureaus chafed at not reporting directly to the secretary and having less status in the hi-
erarchy than the administrators whom Ripley imported. But
their work with bureau directors had been outstanding, Ripley
stated. In turn, these imported people felt privileged to work
for Ripley, even though he could be tough and determined
when dealing with outsiders.

He had little patience for those who challenged him, like
the hotheaded anthropologist Clifford Evans and his Senate
of Scientists. At one key meeting, the *Smithsonian* magazine
writer and editor Edwards Park recalled that Ripley "argued
back amiably" when offered alternatives to his own ideas. At
the conclusion, "Ripley's voice became even gentler and the
well-bred drawl more pronounced. The effect was that the
room stilled and his words came across with unmistakable
clarity."[17] It would be done his way—or not at all.

He kept his eye on many details, sampling the meals to be
served at formal dinners and personally supervising the seat-
ing arrangements. He gave the Institution what David Challinor called "a subtle reflection of his own character" while
"never losing sight of the big picture."[18] He was notoriously
late for meetings, at which he often kept silent until deliver-
ing his opinion at the end. He was not afraid of anything or
anybody.

What worked for him at the Smithsonian had also won him
many accolades and nominations in the broader world. At the
World War II Office of Strategic Services, he was more than
just another spy; he became a ranking diplomat and policy
analyst as well. While other oss officials in Asia put down
Lord Mountbatten as a lightweight, Ripley established a good
working relationship with the theater commander. Ripley

would have made a credible ambassador to Nepal, a position
he briefly sought in the early 1950s with help from Senator
Prescott Bush, the future presidents' father and grandfather.
"This young man would certainly be an excellent person to
consider," wrote the White House fixer and Connecticut governor Sherman Adams in response to Senator Bush's inquiry.[19]
Ripley's hat was also briefly in the ring during the search for a
president of Yale to succeed A. Whitney Griswold, who died
in 1963. Though the Ripley campaign faltered, having been
too little and too late, it aroused interesting speculation about
what Yale would have been like with an activist-scientist at the
helm rather than another scholarly humanist.

Ripley was not a loner. To get the job done, he often formed
fruitful partnerships with powerful or influential others. "He
loved people," the ornithologist Bruce Beehler, a longtime
Ripley assistant, said when we met at his lab, "but especially
those in positions of power, elected or inherited, whom he
often persuaded to support the advancement of science, culture, or conservation."[20] In his student years, Evelyn Hutchinson and Ernst Mayr helped steer Ripley into the world of birds
and the broader importance of studying them.

The Yale grandee Lefty Lewis gave Ripley an introduction to General Donovan and boosted him into the wartime
OSS, and guided him upward on Yale's academic ladder. There
Ripley also established a close friendship with the austere
A. Whitney Griswold during his Yale presidency and felt
bereft when Griswold died and the guard changed. Ripley's
thirty-year partnership with India's Sálim Ali is the clearest
example of how he most liked to work. Another indication
was the team of loyal deputies that he built himself at the
Smithsonian. It should come as no surprise that the Ripleys

established a warm friendship with Joseph and Olga Hirsh-
horn, bringing in the socialite Permelia Reed and the White
House arts adviser Roger Stevens as intermediaries and Lady
Bird Johnson as the compelling siren whistling in the important Hirshhorn art collection. So it was also with Joseph and
Dame Jillian Sackler and with the notoriously demanding
Enid Haupt. Ripley worked closely with Blitzer and Senator
Daniel Patrick Moynihan, who also became a close friend, to
found the Wilson Center. He also called on Moynihan for help
in selling on the Hill a model way, proposed by the ecologist
Tom Lovejoy, to use Third World debt to underwrite nature
conservation activities by means of what became known as
debt-for-nature swaps.

A Sticky Baton

After he retired in 1984, Ripley returned briefly to his previous pursuits as an inveterate traveler and student of birds.
He welcomed the freedom to set his own pace. He thought
about writing a book, similar in style to his Nepal narrative,
on his adventures in remote Bhutan during a family trip in
1973. Finally, after decades of putting time with his ducks onto
the always overloaded calendar, he was able to relax and enjoy
their company. But he keenly wanted to stay busy at the office,
and as emeritus he sometimes acted as if he were still running
the show.

In February 1989, five years after his retirement, he wrote
a chatty letter to the Aga Khan, saying he would soon be in
Paris and proposing a meeting to discuss ways to spread "understanding of the vast cultural resources of the Islamic world"
through S. Dillon Ripley Center activities in the Smithsonian

Quadrangle.[21] He and Mary would be flying home aboard a Concorde airplane that was being donated to the Smithsonian on a schedule that offered the Ripleys a little extra time for that meeting. Nothing happened as a result of the letter, but it stands as an example of the author's determination to remain in touch with powerful and well-heeled people.

As he was settling in to the relatively balmy autumn of his life, in the mid-1980s, Ripley fell while leaving a restaurant in New Haven. Ironically, he had returned to attend a memorial service for his mentor Evelyn Hutchinson. The consequences of that fall were severe, and Ripley never truly recovered from it. His brain damaged, he was stricken with the cruel disorder called aphasia, which left him aware of what was going on around him but deprived him of the power to speak, read, or write. After Mary's death in 1996, he lived at home alone for five final years. David Challinor visited him weekly, passing along fresh news of developments in scientific communities. As Ripley lay dying of pneumonia at the age of eighty-seven in his artifact-strewn Washington home, his daughter Sylvia visited him daily and massaged his hands.

The Style of a Leader

Ripley simply could not ignore opportunities. He loved getting attention. He seldom questioned his own authority and high rank. Early in his career he awakened Yale's Peabody Museum, not to cloak himself in glory or build an empire, but rather to breathe life into what he saw as a weary place with great potential. The same on a far larger scale can be said about his two Smithsonian decades. He liked working with architects and appreciated many branches of architectural history, but what excited him about the bricks and mortar had mostly to do with the knowledge and the skills and the passions to be lodged and displayed from within those new spaces for the benefit of swarming publics. The buildings were means to ends, not ends in themselves.

Though Ripley eagerly sought growth and visibility for the Smithsonian, and attention for himself, he was discriminating about his choices and deftly fended off unwanted suitors. One rejection for budget reasons was Marjorie Merriweather Post's elaborate Hillwood House in northwest Washington's wooded backlands. It felt good, Ripley mused, to say no from time to time, as he did when the Smithsonian was offered the San Francisco Mint and the National Archives with its huge collection. Among other prospective trophies that he turned down were the ss *United States*, the speedy ocean liner, and Howard Hughes's giant wooden "Spruce Goose" seaplane.

He cared every bit as much as James Smithson did about the acquisition and diffusion of knowledge, and early on he could not fancy himself spending a whole career as the Ripley family's staid lawyer. Though not particularly religious, he believed deeply, much as a devoted pastor does, in the notion of service. He was profoundly American and profoundly liberal. He wrapped all his thoughts and instincts into the context of a fragile planet and the undeniable need for worthy science to come to the rescue. And have "great fun" along the way.

In his memoir published in the *Proceedings of the American Philosophical Society*, David Challinor added this discerning note about the man he proudly rated as his mentor for twenty-five years:

> The most fitting way to describe him is to say that he had both class and stature, qualities normally awarded to an individual rather than sought by the recipient. To seek stature pre-

cludes your gaining it. Class is a more ephemeral quality, and is achieved only by years of paying attention to details, and to individuals. His standards were high, but all who worked for him, as well as millions of visitors to the Institution, benefited in some way from exposure to the accomplishments of this extraordinary man.[22]

Taking the long view, the *Washington Post* art and architecture critic Philip Kennicott expressed strong views about Ripley's style. Though the Smithsonian still "reflexively defines itself as American," he wrote, "it has scholars of international reputation, and it should start to imagine itself as an international institution, a worldly cosmopolitan entity that can convene and attract the best minds and take leadership on issues that threaten our survival as a planet and a species." No one would have applauded these words more heartily than Dillon Ripley, crowned by Kennicott as "the embodiment of the institution's best values."[23]

If you were to draw a composite picture with images summarizing the principal components of Ripley's life, a central element would feature science. It would encompass Litchfield and the ducks tugging at Ripley's trousers in search of a snack. There would be Ripley himself on a summer afternoon, at the oars of a little rowboat on the duck pond, wearing an old tweed jacket and a necktie, Mary and two of the daughters aboard as well. There, too, would be Ripley fully costumed for rugged fieldwork in some distant land, astride an elephant's neck, barely concealing his eagerness to discover, or Ripley displaying his impatience upon being told by a Nepalese outfitter that its porters were "taking food, sir, but just now coming." And there as well would be a gallery of the towering figures, starting perhaps with Darwin, whose work had encouraged him to abandon a conventional life and clamber upward on Yale's

Science Hill and on the Mall. The skin of a rare bird would complete the picture.

For this insatiable omnivore, great satisfaction could be derived from all of the above. No one had more fun, or worked harder, at the task of increasing and diffusing knowledge.

Acknowledgments

"It's a crying need," said the Smithsonian veteran Marc Pachter when I told him I was working on a book about Dillon Ripley. He and others noted that, though the archives have an abundance of autobiographical material, third-party coverage of the full span of Ripley's life is in short supply. The *New Yorker* writer Geoffrey T. Hellman produced a fine profile in 1950. Various other media — the *Washington Post* and the *Washington Star*, the *Hartford Courant* — published profiles. Obituary pages gave Ripley ample space. But no one had yet gone through the archive box by box, folder by folder to assemble a more complete analysis of this man's remarkable record and how it evolved.

Starting out on my journey, I quickly found that most of those who had worked closely with Ripley were no longer with us, though there were a few exceptions. The foreign affairs practitioner Fisher Howe, who served under Ripley in the World War II Office of Strategic Services, was able to offer crisp memories a few days before his hundredth birthday. Ripley's events producer, Wilton Dillon (no relative), was just as articulate at age ninety-two. Paul Perrot had sharp and pleasant memories of his years as Ripley's principal museum professional. Tom Lovejoy, helpful as ever, offered sage advice across a broad spectrum, and warm memories, as well as this book's much-appreciated foreword.

As for the rest, I had to rely in large measure on the rich

trove of oral history materials that Ripley and others left behind. Especially useful was the set of forty audiotaped conversations with Ripley, most of them an hour or more in length.
Almost all of them were transcribed, and those between 1977
and 1993 were compiled by Pamela M. Henson of the Smithsonian Institution Archives. My thanks to Ms. Henson for
all she did to make these materials available to me and for
commenting on portions of my manuscript. Ellen Alers of the
same department was another valued member of the archival
research team.

Elsewhere at the far-flung Smithsonian, there were many
friendly faces. I especially appreciated the time spent with the
ornithologist Bruce Beehler, who shares the enthusiasm Ripley had for the splendid birds of New Guinea and showed me
the lab to which Ripley retreated when he could. Two other
former Ripley assistants, Roger Pasquier and Warren King,
offered warm thoughts. Amy Ballard and Rick Stamm supplied rich insight into the heart of the Smithsonian Castle.
James Goode, George Watson, Carey Winfrey, Mary White,
Phil Cook, Sally Maran, and Geoffrey La Riche all provided
help. Dodge Thompson at the National Gallery of Art offered
thoughts about the sometimes tense relationship between
Ripley and the Gallery. Maygene Daniels, Anne Ritchie, and
Jean Henry of the National Gallery Archive proffered backup
materials. Cynthia Helms and Janet McClelland provided
spirited thoughts about Washington's Ripley-era cultural and
social scene.

As for Yale, a former director of the Peabody Museum,
Derek Briggs, took an interest in the project and gave me helpful entrée to others, including the ornithologists Rick Prum
and Kristof Zyskowski. The latter proudly presented Yale's

carefully maintained bird collection and carefully tagged examples of how Ripley fortified it. The staff of the Livingston Ripley Waterfowl Conservancy in Litchfield showed me and my family handsome ducks of many species. Charlie Roraback, a Yale classmate, drove me around and introduced me to Catherine Keene Fields, the cheerful director of the Litchfield Historical Society.

At my Washington office, the landlady, Grace Guggenheim, and her staff cheerfully provided invaluable extra services. So did my officemates down the hall, staff members of the Washington-based Bhutan Foundation: Bruce Bunting, Tshewang Wangchuk, Dawa Sherpa, and Tshering Yangzom, who, groaning, unfailingly responded to my plaintive queries about computer issues simple to them but beyond analog-minded me. Georgie Warner and Sylvia Ripley Addison combed the archives in search of the best among countless photographs to accompany the text.

Over the three-year life of the project, greatly needed financial support was received from numerous sources, including Christopher Addison, Douglas Banker, Wendy Benchley, William Bernhard and Catherine Cahill, Eleanor Briggs, Joan Challinor, William H. Draper III and Phyllis Draper, Alexander Farman-Farmaian, Elinor Farquhar, Hart Fessenden, Sally Fleming, Lee Folger and Juliet Folger, Aileen T. Geddes, Robert J. Geniesse, Nelse L. Greenway, Anita G. Herrick, David P. Hunt, Freeborn G. Jewett, Jr., Robert Leeson, Jr., John D. Macomber, Nicholas Millhouse, Gail Moloney, Gail Ostergaard, Rosemary Ripley, Sylvia Ripley, Hamilton Robinson, Jr., John Shober, Simon Sidamon-Eristoff, and Elsa Williams.

I owe great gratitude also to two gifted advisers who did much to improve the quality of this book: the editor and historical researcher Skip Moskey and the editorial consultant Colleen Daly; agent Carol Mann also helped a lot throughout the process. Doing the book with them was hard work; I cannot imagine doing it without their treasured assistance.

My wife, Flo, to whom this book is lovingly dedicated, helped in myriad ways. She, in the manner of Dillon Ripley, never gives up.

Roger D. Stone
Washington, DC
December 2015

Chronology

1913	Born (September 20) in New York City
1932	Graduated from St. Paul's School, Concord, New Hampshire
1936	Graduated from Yale University, BA (history)
1936–39	Zoological collector, Philadelphia Academy of Sciences
1936–40	Voluntary assistant, American Museum of Natural History, New York
1939–40	Graduate student and teaching assistant, Harvard University (zoology)
1942	Assistant curator of birds, US National Museum, Washington, DC
1942	Made a member, American Ornithologists' Union
1942–45	Office of Strategic Services, staff member in Washington, DC, and director, Intelligence Operations, Southeast Asia
1943	Harvard University, PhD, zoology
1946–64	Teacher, Yale University
1947	*Trail of the Money Bird* published by Longmans, Green & Co.

1949   Married Mary Moncrieffe Livingston (August 18)

1950   Fulbright Fellow

1951   Made a fellow, American Ornithologists' Union

1952   *Search for the Spiny Babbler* published by Victor Gollancz Ltd.

1954   Guggenheim Fellow

1957   *A Paddling of Ducks* published by Harcourt Brace & Co.

1958–82   President, International Council for Bird Preservation

1959–64   Director, Peabody Museum of Natural History, Yale University

1964–84   Secretary, Smithsonian Institution, Washington, DC

1966   Awarded gold medal, New York Zoological Society

1968–   *Handbook of the Birds of India and Pakistan* with Sálim Ali, ten volumes, published by Oxford University Press

1969   *The Sacred Grove: Essays on Museums* published by Simon & Schuster

1977   *Rails of the World* published by David R. Godine

1981–88   Chairman, US Board of Directors, World Wildlife Fund

1985   Received Presidential Medal of Freedom

2001   Died (March 12) in Washington, DC

Notes

Introduction

1. Personal conversation, April 28, 2014.
2. Dillon Ripley, *The Sacred Grove* (New York: Simon & Schuster, 1969), 95.

1. Growing Up Golden

1. Dillon Ripley, Smithsonian Institution Archives, Oral History Program, Interview 1 with Pamela Henson, 3. Chief among the sources of information on Ripley's life and career is the compendium of materials gathered by the Smithsonian Institution Archives under the title "Record Unit 009591." This accumulation, neatly packaged in nine large boxes broken down into individual folders, includes "correspondence, diaries, calendars, itineraries, manuscripts, reprints, news clippings, maps, photographs, and drawings of fauna." The subject matter spans a broad range from banal to exotic: from restringing a tennis racket to buying a cockatoo, from records of correspondence during Ripley's years at the Office of Strategic Services to a discussion of bird feed prices with a supplier.

Separately filed under Record Unit 009591 is a mostly transcribed set of forty audiotaped interviews with Ripley that were conducted and compiled between 1977 and 1993 by Pamela Henson of the Smithsonian Institution Archives' Oral History Program. This unit of the Smithsonian Archives also consists of transcribed oral history interviews with other key people who worked at the Smithsonian under Ripley, notably his chief deputy, Charles Blitzer. After he left the Smithsonian, his health declining, Ripley began writing his own memoirs, but this project never got far along. Much of what he drafted is written in his barely legible handwriting or copied onto smudgy paper.

2. Dillon Ripley, Smithsonian Institution Archives, Oral History Program, Interview 1, 3.

3. Ibid., 5.

4. Ibid., 6.

5. Ibid., 13, 16.

6. Ibid., 18.

7. Ibid., 17.

8. Ibid., 18.

9. Dillon Ripley, Smithsonian Institution Archives, Oral History Program, Interview 2, 21–22.

10. Ibid., 24.

11. Ibid., 37, 39.

12. Dillon Ripley, Smithsonian Institution Archives, Oral History Program, Interview 3, 42.

13. Ibid., 43.

14. Ibid., 45.

15. Ibid.

16. Ibid., 53.

17. Ibid., 65, 67–68.

18. Dillon Ripley, Smithsonian Institution Archives, Oral History Program, Interview 4, 70.

19. Ibid., 77–80.

20. Ibid., 90.

21. Dillon Ripley, *A Paddling of Ducks* (New York: Harcourt, Brace, 1957), 44.

22. Ripley, Oral History Program, Interview 4, 98–99.

2. *Birds of Many Feathers*

1. Rollin G. Osterweis, *Three Centuries of New Haven* (New Haven, CT: Yale University Press, 1953), 421.

2. Ibid., 423.

3. Dillon Ripley, Draft memoirs, Smithsonian Institution Archives, Collection 7008, Box 110, Part 1, Version B, 24.

4. Dillon Ripley, *Trail of the Money Bird* (London: Longmans, Green, 1947), xiii.

5. Dillon Ripley, *A Paddling of Ducks* (New York: Harcourt, Brace, 1957), 67.

6. Geoffrey Hellman, "Curator Getting Around," *New Yorker*, August 26, 1950, 31–40.

7. Ripley, *Trail of the Money Bird*, xiii.

8. Hellman, "Curator," 40.

9. Ripley, *Trail of the Money Bird*, xiii.

10. Ibid., xiv.

11. Dillon Ripley, Smithsonian Institution Archives, Oral History Program, Interview 18, 445.

12. Ripley, *Trail of the Money Bird*, 34, 45.

13. Ibid., 205.

14. Ibid., 202–7.

15. Ibid., 204.

16. Dillon Ripley, Smithsonian Institution Archives, Oral History Program, Interview 21, 535–36.

17. Ripley, *Trail of the Money Bird*, 311.

18. Ibid., 223, 281–82.

19. Ibid., xiii, 106.

20. Ibid., 334.

21. Ibid.

22. John Ketcham, Letter to Dillon Ripley, June 20, 1939, Smithsonian Institution Archives, Collection 7008, Box 6, Folder: Vanderbilt-1, 8, 4.

23. George Vanderbilt, Letter to Dillon Ripley, May 5, 1939, Smithsonian Institution Archives, Collection 7008, Box 6, Folder: Vanderbilt-2, 6.

24. Ripley, *A Paddling of Ducks*, 102.

25. Dillon Ripley, Draft memoirs, Smithsonian Institution Archives, Collection 7008, Box 110, Part 1, Version A, 2.

26. Ripley, *Trail of the Money Bird*, 90.

3. Asian and Other Adventures

1. Geoffrey T. Hellman, "Curator Getting Around," *New Yorker*, August 26, 1950, 41.

2. Dillon Ripley, Draft memoirs, Smithsonian Institution Archives, Collection 7008, Box 110, Part 1,Version A, 4.

3. Ibid., 3.

4. Ibid., 7.

5. Ripley, Draft memoirs, Part 1, Version A, 9.

6. Ibid., 10.

7. Ibid.

8. Dillon Ripley, Draft memoirs, Smithsonian Institution Archives, Collection 7008, Box 110, Part 1, Version B, 16.

9. Robert Murphy, *Diplomat Among Warriors* (New York: Doubleday, 1964), 90.

10. Godfrey Hodgson: "Yale—A Great Nursery of Spooks," *New York Times*, August 16, 1987.

11. Ripley, Draft memoirs, Part 1, Version B, Part 2, 19.

12. Dillon Ripley, Draft memoirs, Smithsonian Institution Archives, Collection 7008, Box 110, Part 2, Version A, 46.

13. Ripley, Draft memoirs, Part 1, Version A, 3.

14. Ripley, Draft memoirs, Part 1, Version B, 21.

15. Dillon Ripley, Draft memoirs, Smithsonian Institution Archives, Collection 7008, Box 110, Part 2, Version B, 14.

16. Ripley, Draft memoirs, Part 2, Version A, 36.

17. Ibid., 48.

18. Ibid., 49.

19. Dillon Ripley, Draft memoirs, Smithsonian Institution Archives, Collection 7008, Box 110, Part 3, Version C, 49.

20. Ibid., page numbers missing.

21. Ripley, Draft memoirs, Part 2, Version A, 48.

22. E. Bruce Reynolds, *Thailand's Secret War* (Cambridge: Cambridge University Press, 2005), xv.

23. Bob Bergin, "OSS and Free Thai Operations in World War II," *Studies in Intelligence* 55, no. 4, Extracts (December 2011), 11.

24. Ibid., 12.

25. Dillon Ripley, "Incident in Siam," *Yale Review*, no. 36 (Winter 1947), 276.

26. Ibid., 264–65.

27. Hellman, "Curator," 42.

28. Reynolds, *Thailand's Secret War*, xvi.

29. Bergin, "OSS and Free Thai Operations," 11.

30. Dillon Ripley, *A Paddling of Ducks* (New York: Harcourt, Brace, 1957), 152.

31. Whitney H. Shepardson, Letter to Dillon Ripley, March 3, 1944, Smithsonian Institution Archives, Collection 7008, Box 10, Folder 7, 1.

32. General William Donovan, Letter to Dillon Ripley, October 1, 1945, Smithsonian Institution Archives, Collection 7008, Box 10, Folder 4, 1.

33. Ripley, "Incident in Siam," 276.

4. Pleasantly Busy in New Haven

1. Dillon Ripley, Smithsonian Institution Archives, Oral History Program, Interview 17, 431.

2. Geoffrey Hellman, "Curator Getting Around," *New Yorker*, August 26, 1950, 42, 47.

3. Nancy G. Slack, *G. Evelyn Hutchinson and the Invention of Modern Ecology* (New Haven, CT: Yale University Press, 2010), 1.

4. Ibid.

5. Dillon Ripley, Smithsonian Institution Archives, Oral History Program, Interview 18, 449.

6. Dillon Ripley, Smithsonian Institution Archives, Oral History Program, Interview 20, 514.

7. Michael Lewis, *Inventing Global Ecology* (Athens: Ohio University Press, 2004), 33.

8. Ibid., 48.

9. Dillon Ripley, Smithsonian Institution Archives, Oral History Program, Interview 21, 534–37.

10. Lewis, *Inventing Global Ecology*, 74.

11. Dillon Ripley, *A Paddling of Ducks* (New York: Harcourt, Brace, 1957), 158, 143, 168.

12. Dillon Ripley, *Search for the Spiny Babbler* (London: Victor Gollancz, 1953), 4–5.

13. Ibid., 5.

14. Lewis, *Inventing Global Ecology*, 86, 87.

15. Ripley, *Search for the Spiny Babbler*, 9, 16.

16. Ibid., 93.

17. Ibid., 114.

18. Ibid., 285, 286–87.

19. Ibid., 149.

20. Ibid., 288.

21. Phil Casey, "Ripley: He's Fun to Go Walking With," *Washington Post*, May 25, 1969.

22. Ripley, *A Paddling of Ducks*, 122.

23. Dillon Ripley, "Waterfowl in a Country Place," Unpublished paper, Smithsonian Institution Archives, RU7008, Folder 4, 3.

24. Casey, "Ripley: He's Fun to Go Walking With."

25. There are several sources of information in this paragraph: Dillon Ripley, Smithsonian Institution Archives, Oral History Program, Interview 22, 569–71 and Interview 23, 577–80; Personal communication from Rosemary Ripley, June 2014.

26. C. Evelyn Hutchinson, Letter to Rebecca West, August 11, 1963, Hutchinson Papers, University of Tulsa, as quoted by Nancy G. Slack.

5. Defining a New Culture

1. Russell Baker, "It's Middletown on the Potomac," *New York Times Magazine*, February 14, 1965. Excerpted in Katherine Graham, ed., *Katherine Graham's Washington* (New York: Alfred A. Knopf, 2002), 48.

2. Dillon Ripley, "Statement by the Secretary," *Smithsonian Year 1984*, 8.

3. Shelby Coffey, "Take Note of Smithsonian Associates," *Washington Post*, March 23, 1969.

4. Dillon Ripley, "Broader Audience Asked for Kennedy Center Planners," Letter cited in *Washington Post*, December 19, 1965.

5. James Morris, *Smithsonian Impresario* (self-published, 2010), ch. 4, 14.

6. Dillon Ripley, Smithsonian Institution Archives, Oral History Program, Interview 35, 20.

7. Peter Yarrow, Foreword to *Folk City: New York and the American Folk Music Revival*, Stephen Petrus and Ronald D. Cohen, eds. (New York: Oxford University Press, 2015), 10.

8. Dillon Ripley, "Statement by the Secretary," *Smithsonian Year 1967*, 32.

9. Ripley, Oral History Program, Interview 35, 37.

10. Morris, *Smithsonian Impresario*, 171–72.

11. Dillon Ripley, "The Ides of March to Have Our National Pride," Opening remarks at the seventh annual Festival of American Folklife, 1974 (attribution illegible in Smithsonian Archives SDR folder).

12. William S. Walker, *A Living Exhibition* (Amherst: University of Massachusetts Press, 2013), 101.

13. Ibid., 153–95.

14. Rita Burnham and Elliott Kai-Kee, *Teaching in the Art Museum* (Los Angeles: Getty Publications, 2013), 42.

15. Walker, *A Living Exhibition*, 116.

16. Dillon Ripley, Smithsonian Institution Archives, Oral History Program, Interview 31, 8–9.

17. Ibid., 9.

18. Dillon Ripley, *The Sacred Grove: Essays on Museums* (New York: Simon & Shuster, 1969), 107.

19. Caryl Marsh, "A Neighborhood Museum That Works," *Museum News*, October 1968, 14.

20. Walker, *A Living Exhibition*, 121–22.

21. Ripley, *The Sacred Grove*, 111.

22. Dillon Ripley, Smithsonian Institution Archives, Oral History Program, Interview 32, 9–20.

23. Ibid., 12.

6. Displaying the Nation's Art

1. Paul H. Oehser, *The Smithsonian Institution*, rev. ed. (Boulder, CO: Westview Press, 1983), 22.

2. Ibid., 103.

3. Charles Peters, *Lyndon B. Johnson* (New York: Henry Holt, 2010), 8.

4. Dillon Ripley, Lyndon Baines Johnson Library, Oral history interview, October 4, 1974, 4.

5. Philip Kennicott, "The Great Society at 50," *Washington Post*, May 20, 2014.

6. Aline Saarinen, *The Proud Possessors* (New York: Random House, 1958), 269–86.

7. Ibid.

8. Dillon Ripley, Smithsonian Institution Archives, Oral History Program, Interview 25, 624.

9. Ibid., 628.

10. Ripley, Oral history interview, October 4, 1974, 4.

11. Ripley, Oral History Program, Interview 25, 625.

12. Dillon Ripley, Letter to Richard Goodwin, July 25, 1965, Smithsonian Institution Archives, Collection 99, Box 114, Folder [5].

13. Dillon Ripley, Letter to Mrs. Johnson, November 22, 1965, Smithsonian Institution Archives, Collection 99, Box 114, Folder [5].

14. Dillon Ripley, Smithsonian Institution Archives, Oral History Program, Interview 26, 643.

15. Sally Quinn, "Hirshhorn II: Night of the Important Ones," *Washington Post*, October 3, 1974; Paul Richard, "Assessing the Hirshhorn Museum on the Eve of Its Opening," *Washington Post*, September 29, 1974; Ada Louise Huxtable, [no title], *New York Times*, October 6, 1974.

16. Richard, "Assessing the Hirshhorn Museum."

17. Ibid.

18. Ripley, Oral History Program, Interview 26, 638.

19. Franklin Murphy, National Gallery of Art, Oral History Program, Interview conducted by A. C. Viebranz, January 24 and May 2, 1990.

20. Paul Mellon with John Baskett, *Reflections in a Silver Spoon* (New York: William Morrow, 1992), 305.

21. Ripley, Oral History Program, Interview 26, 645.

22. Dillon Ripley, Smithsonian Institution Archives, Oral History Program, Interview 28, 703.

23. Elizabeth Foy, National Gallery of Art, Oral History Program, Interview conducted by John J. Harter, May 15 and 16, 1989, 149.

24. Ripley, Oral History Program, Interview 25, 618–19.

25. Paul Richard, "Gallery Head David Scott Quits," *Washington Post*, May 10, 1969.

26. Ripley, Oral History Program, Interview 28, 688.

27. Paul Richard, "Archives for Art," *Washington Post*, May 5, 1970.

28. Mellon, *Reflections in a Silver Spoon*, 303.

29. Ripley, Oral History Program, Interview 28, 705.

30. Ibid., 701–2.

31. Charles Blitzer, Memorandum to Dillon Ripley, Smithsonian Institution Archives, Collection 99, Box 394, Folder 137, April 8, 1970.

32. Mellon, *Reflections in a Silver Spoon*, 305.

33. J. Carter Brown, Letter to Dillon Ripley, October 10, 1969, National Gallery of Art Archives, Collection 99, Box 327, Folder [1].

7. *Media Ventures and Scholarly Triumph*

1. Dillon Ripley, Letter to Edwin Foster Blair, Jr., et al., October 26, 1952, Smithsonian Institution Archives, Box 8, Reports 48–62.

2. As reported by Eric Pace, "E. K. Thompson, 89, Editor Who Shaped *Life* Magazine," *New York Times*, October 9, 1996.

3. Carey Winfrey, "Curveballs at the Un-Magazine," *Smithsonian*, April 2010.

4. Ibid.

5. Edward K. Thompson, *A Love Affair with LIFE & Smithsonian* (Columbia: University of Missouri Press, 1995), 257, 259.

6. Ibid., 259, 260.

7. Ibid., 262.

8. Ibid.

9. Ibid., 263.

10. Ibid, 263.

11. Edward K. Thompson, Memorandum to Dillon Ripley, January 23, 1969, the author's files.

12. Edward K. Thompson, Memorandum to staff, May 8, 1969, the author's files.

13. Thompson, *Love Affair*, 272.

14. Ibid., 267, 266.

15. Edwards Park, quoted in Carey Winfrey, "Noxious Bugs and Amorous Elephants," *Smithsonian*, November 2005.

16. Ibid., 260.

17. *Newsweek* (1973), as cited in Carey Winfrey, "Curveballs at the Un-Magazine," *Smithsonian*, June 24, 2010.

18. Quoted in Jim Romenseko, "Smithsonian Editor Announces Retirement," *Washington Post*, April 8, 2011.

19. Ibid.

20. Winfrey, "Noxious Bogs and Amorous Elephants."

21. Dillon Ripley, Smithsonian Institution Archives, Oral History Program, Interview 34, 2.

22. Ibid.

23. Ibid, 3–4.

24. Charles Blitzer, Smithsonian Institution Archives, Oral History Program, Interview, 64.

25. Ripley, Oral History Program, Interview 34, 6.

26. Dillon Ripley, "Statement by the Secretary," *Smithsonian Year 1970*, 3.

27. Ripley, Oral History Program, Interview 34, 8.

28. Ibid.

29. Ripley, "Statement by the Secretary," *Smithsonian Year 1970*, 3.

30. Ibid.

31. Charles Blitzer, Smithsonian Institution Archives, Oral History Program, Interview, 32.

32. Dillon Ripley, "Statement by the Secretary," *Smithsonian Year 1969*, 5.

8. Building Smithsonian U.

1. Dillon Ripley, *The Sacred Grove* (New York: Simon & Schuster, 1969), 85.

2. Dillon Ripley, "Statement by the Secretary," *Smithsonian Year 1966*, 1.

3. Dillon Ripley, "Statement by the Secretary," *Smithsonian Year 1967*, 5.

4. Claude Lévi-Strauss, "Anthropology: Its Achievements and Future," *Knowledge Among Men* (New York: Simon & Schuster, 1966), 113.

5. Dillon Ripley, "Statement by the Secretary," *Smithsonian Year 1982*, 6.

6. Dillon Ripley, Dr. Arthur M. Sackler Special Issue, *Studio International* 200, Suppl. 1, September 1,1987, 18.

7. Arthur M. Sackler, Cited in *Arthur M. Sackler*, Miguel Angel Benavides Lopez, producer, Michael Patrick Hearn, ed. (AMS Foundation, 2012), 100.

8. Sonia Reece, "The Making of a Museum," in *The Smithsonian: 150 Years of Adventure, Discovery, and Wonder*, James Conaway, ed. (New York: Alfred A. Knopf, 1995), 366.

9. Ripley, Dr. Arthur M. Sackler Special Issue, 18.

10. Amy Ballard, "Synopsis of Development of the Quadrangle Complex," Background paper, Smithsonian Institution, 2015.

11. Henry F. du Pont, Memorandum to the Secretary and Regents of the Smithsonian Institution, January 20, 1965, Smithsonian Institution Archives, Collection 613, Box 60, Folder [1], 12.

12. Dillon Ripley, Draft of letter to Cooper Hewitt, Board Chair, and Arthur A. Houghton, Jr., Smithsonian Institution Archives, Collection 613, Box 60, Folder [1].

13. Ibid.

14. Dillon Ripley, Memorandum to Senator Claiborne Pell, September 18, 1974, Smithsonian Institution Archives, Collection 613, Box 243, Folder [1], 8–9.

15. Dillon Ripley, *The Sacred Grove* (New York: Simon & Schuster, 1969), 79.

16. Ibid.

17. Ripley, "Statement by the Secretary," *Smithsonian Year 1967*, 6.

18. Dillon Ripley, Letter to David Challinor, August 8, 1975, Smithsonian Institution Archives, Collection 613, Box 432, Folder [Mall/Last Site 1975], 1.

19. Dillon Ripley, Memorandum to the Executive Committee, Smithsonian Institution, November 8, 1974, Smithsonian Institution Archives, Collection 615, Box 432, Folder [M of M], 1.

20. *Congressional Record*, December 23, 1969, Smithsonian Institution Archives, Collection 99, Box 371, Folder [M of M.], H.R. 15429.

21. Dillon Ripley, Memorandum to Smithsonian Regents, November 8, 1974, Smithsonian Institution Archives, Collection 613, Box 432, Folder [M of M].

22. David Challinor, Memorandum to Mr. S. D. Ripley, September 28, 1977, Smithsonian Institution Archives, Collection 613, Box 404, Folder [M of M], 1.

23. Dillon Ripley, "Statement by the Secretary," *Smithsonian Year 1972*, 11.

24. Dillon Ripley, "Statement by the Secretary," *Smithsonian Year 1974*, 9.

25. William S. Walker, *A Living Exhibition* (Amherst: University of Massachusetts Press, 2013), 209.

26. Senator Barry Goldwater, "Time of Crisis for the National Air and Space Museum," May 19, 1970, *Congressional Record*, Vol. 116, Part 12, 16095.

9. Waves of Complaints

1. Smithsonian Institution Announcement, August 4, 1970, Gallery Archives, ZC1, J. Carter Brown Subject Files, Box 84, Museums Hearings, July 1970, National Gallery of Art.

2. Kenneth Turan, [no title], *Washington Post*, January 6, 1974.

3. Editors of the *Falmouth Enterprise* [now the *Cape Cod Times*], "Fight with Sense of Humor," copy in the author's files.

4. Letters to the Editor, *Washington Post*, June 9, 1973.

5. Robert H. Simmons, Letter to J. William Fulbright, November 26, 1969, Smithsonian Institution Archives, Collection 99, Box 459, Folder [C13], Simmons, 1.

6. Dillon Ripley, Letter to the Honorable J. William Fulbright, December 15, 1969, Smithsonian Institution Archives, Collection 99, Box 459, 1.

7. Robert H. Simmons, Letter to Warren Burger, October 10, 1969, Smithsonian Institution Archives, Collection 99, Box 459, Folder [C12], Misc. Simmons, 1.

8. Robert H. Simmons, Letter to Warren Burger, October 7, 1969, Smithsonian Institution Archives, Collection 99, Box 459, Folder [C12], Misc. Simmons, 1.

9. Ibid., 2.

10. Dillon Ripley, Letter to Warren Burger, October 15, 1969, Smithsonian Institution Archives, Collection 99, Box 459, Folder [1], Misc. Simmons, 1.

11. Dillon Ripley, Letter to the Honorable Clinton P. Anderson, November 19, 1969, Smithsonian Institution Archives, Collection 99, Box 459, Folder [1], Misc. Simmons, 1.

12. Dillon Ripley, Confidential statement to the Honorable Clinton P. Anderson, February 5, 1970, Smithsonian Institution Archives, Collection 99, Box 447, Folder [Misc. Simmons, Robert 1970], 5.

13. Robert Simmons, Letter to Chief Justice Burger, October 9, 1969, Smithsonian Institution Archives, Collection 99, Box 459, Folder [1], Misc. Simmons, 2.

14. Roger Stevens, Letter to the *New York Times*, May 22, 1970.

15. Jack Anderson, "Coca-Cola Set to Defend Franchises," *Washington Post*, November 27, 1972.

16. Jack Anderson, "$2,800 Search for a Gull," *Washington Post*, November 23, 1969.

17. Clifford Evans, Senate of Scientists Project, Smithsonian Institution Archives, Oral History Project, Interview, May 28, 1975, 66, 59.

18. Philip M. Kadis, "Plucking Pelicans at the Smithsonian," *Washington Star*, June 26, 1977.

19. Jack Anderson, "Nixon Foundation Skimps on Charity," *Washington Post*, August 2, 1974.

20. Thomas J. Watson, Jr., Letter to Dr. S. Dillon Ripley, August 26, 1970, Smithsonian Institution Archives, Collection 99, Box 369, Folder [4], SI Legislation (July 1970 Hearings), 1.

21. Philip S. Humphrey, "An Ecological Survey of the Central Pacific," Annual Report of the Smithsonian Institution, 1965, 24.

22. Ted Gup, "The Smithsonian Secret," *Washington Post Magazine*, May 12, 1985, 9.

23. Roy MacLeod, "Strictly for the Birds: Science, the Military, and the Smithsonian's Pacific Ocean Biological Survey Program, 1963–1970," *Journal of the History of Biology* 34 (2001), 315–52.

24. Gup, "Smithsonian Secret," 17.

25. Ibid., 14.

26. MacLeod, "Strictly for the Birds," 343–44.

10. Science and Conservation

1. Dillon Ripley, "Statement by the Secretary," *Smithsonian Year 1967*, 3.

2. Dillon Ripley, "Conservation in Developing Countries," Keynote address, Bombay Natural History Society Centenary Seminar, December 1983, Smithsonian Institution Archives, Collection 7008, Box 61, Folder "Centenary," 3–5.

3. Dillon Ripley, Interview for *Point Reyes Bird Observatory Newsletter*, 1981, Smithsonian Institution Archives, Collection 92-063, Box 7, Publications (2), 3.

4. Dillon Ripley, Smithsonian Institution Archives, Oral History Program, Interview 36, 4.

5. Ibid., 5.

6. Dillon Ripley, Smithsonian Institution Archives, Oral History Program, Interview 35, 7.

7. Ibid., 7, 10.

8. Statement attributed to Tony Beamish, cited in Nancy Slack, *G. Evelyn Hutchinson and the Invention of Modern Ecology* (New Haven, CT: Yale University Press 2010), 317.

11. Retiring the Crown

1. Joyce Hoffman, "The Rarest Bird," *Hartford Courant*, October 25, 1987.

2. Dillon Ripley, "Statement by the Secretary," *Smithsonian Year 1984*, 25, 28.

3. Ibid., 16.

4. Ibid.

5. Ibid., 13.

6. Ibid., 10.

7. Wolf Von Eckardt, "The Capital's Dashing Suitor of Culture," *Washington Star*, October 23, 1966.

8. Charles Blitzer, Quoted by James Conaway, *The Smithsonian, 150 Years of Adventure Discovery, and Wonder* (New York: Alfred A. Knopf / Washington, DC: Smithsonian Books, 1995), 378.

9. Sally Maran, Telephone interview with the author, Spring 2015.

10. Mary White, Telephone message to the author, 1983.

11. Paul Perrot, Interview with the author, Spring 2015.

12. Marc Pachter, Personal communication with the author, Fall 2013.

13. Sylvia Ripley Addison, Interview with the author, Summer 2014.

14. Paul Perrot, Interview with the author, Spring 2015.

15. Charles Blitzer, Smithsonian Institution Archives, Oral History Program, Interview 1, Collection 9604, Box 1, 24–25.

16. David Challinor, "S. Dillon Ripley," *Proceedings of the American Philosophical Society* 147, No. 3 (September 2003), 301.

17. Edwards Park, "Secretary S. Dillon Ripley Retires after Twenty Years of Innovation," *Smithsonian*, September 1984, 78.

18. Challinor, "S. Dillon Ripley," 300.

19. Sherman Adams, Letter to Prescott Bush, June 10, 1953, Smithsonian Institution Archives, Collection 7008, Box 7, Folder B.

20. Bruce Beehler, Interview with the author, Winter 2014.

21. Dillon Ripley, Letter to His Highness the Aga Khan, February 15, 1989, Smithsonian Institution Archives, Collection 7008, Box 92, Folder "France," 1.

22. Challinor, "S. Dillon Ripley," 301.

23. Philip Kennicott, "What the Smithsonian Needs in a Leader," *Washington Post*, December 13, 2013.

Bibliography

Bartholomew-Feis, Dixee R. *The OSS and Ho Chi Minh: Unexpected Allies in the War Against Japan.* Lawrence: Kansas University Press, 2006.

Beehler, Bruce. *A Naturalist in New Guinea.* Austin: University of Texas Press, 1991.

Beehler, Bruce, Roger F. Pasquier, and Warren B. King. "In Memoriam, S. Dillon Ripley." *Auk* 119, no. 4 (2002): 1110–13.

Bergin, Bob. "OSS and Free Thai Operations in World War II." *Studies in Intelligence* 55, no. 4 (December 2011): 11–22.

Burnham, Rika, and Elliott Kai-Kee. *Teaching in the Art Museum: Interpretation as Experience.* Los Angeles: J. Paul Getty Museum, 2011.

Challinor, David. "S. Dillon Ripley, 20 September 1913–12 March 2001." *Proceedings of the American Philosophical Society* 147, no. 3 (September 2003): 297–302.

Conaway, James. *The Smithsonian: 150 Years of Adventure, Discovery and Wonder.* New York: Alfred E. Knopf, 1995.

Cruickshank, Charles. *SOE in the Far East.* Oxford: Oxford University Press, 1983.

Dillon, Wilton. *Smithsonian Stories: Chronicle of a Golden Age, 1964–84.* New Brunswick, NJ: Transaction Press, 2015.

Ewing, Heather. *The Lost World of James Smithson.* London: Bloomsbury, 2007.

Ewing, Heather, and Amy Ballard. *A Guide to Smithsonian Architecture.* Washington, DC: Smithsonian Books, 2009.

Graham, Katharine, ed. *Katharine Graham's Washington.* New York: Alfred A. Knopf, 2002.

Harris, Neil. *Capital Culture.* Chicago: Chicago University Press, 2013.

Hellman, Geoffrey T. "Curator for Getting Around." *New Yorker*, August 26, 1950, 31–49.

———. *The Smithsonian: Octopus on the Mall*. New York: Lippincott, 1966.

Henson, Pamela M. Oral History Interviews of S. Dillon Ripley (1997–1993). Smithsonian Institution Archives, Record Unit 009591.

Henwood, Doug. "Spooks in Blue." *Grand Street* (Spring 1988).

Hurrell, Andrew, and Benedict Kingsbury. *The International Politics of the Environment: Actors, Interests, and Institutions*. Oxford: Oxford University Press, 1992.

Lardner, James. "S. Dillon Ripley, Keeper of the Castle." *Washington Post*, November 7, 1982.

Lewis, Michael L. *Inventing Global Ecology: Tracking the Biodiversity Ideal in India, 1947–1997*. Athens: Ohio University Press, 2004.

Mellon, Paul, with John Baskett. *Reflections in a Silver Spoon*. New York: William Morrow, 1992.

Morris, James. *Smithsonian Impresario*. Self-published, 2010.

Oehser, Paul, *The Smithsonian Institution*. Boulder, CO: Westview Press, 1970.

Osterweis, Rollin G. *Three Centuries of New Haven*. New Haven, CT: Yale University Press, 1953.

Reynolds, E. Bruce. *Thailand's Secret War: OSS, SOE, and the Free Thai Underground During World War II*. Cambridge: Cambridge University Press, 2005.

Ripley, Dillon. "Incident in Siam." *Yale Review* 56 (Winter 1947): 262–76.

———. *A Paddling of Ducks*. New York: Harcourt Brace, 1957.

———. *The Sacred Grove: Essays on Museums*. New York: Simon & Schuster, 1969.

———. *Search for the Spiny Babbler: Bird Hunting in Nepal*. London: Victor Gollancz, 1952.

———. Smithsonian Institution Archives, RU 7008, S. Dillon Ripley Papers.

———. *Trail of the Money Bird.* London: Longmans, 1947.

———. US National Archives, Record Group 226, OSS Files.

Ripley, Dillon, and Sálim Ali. *Handbook of the Birds of India and Pakistan.* New York: Oxford University Press, 1974.

Saarinen, Aline B. *The Proud Possessors.* New York: Random House, 1958.

Skelly, David K., David M. Post, and Melinda D. Smith, eds. *The Art of Ecology: Writings of G. Evelyn Hutchinson.* New Haven, CT: Yale University Press, 2010.

Slack, Nancy G. *G. Evelyn Hutchinson and the Invention of Modern Ecology.* New Haven, CT: Yale University Press, 2010.

Smith, Nicol, and Blake Clark. *Into Siam, Underground Kingdom.* New York: Bobbs-Merrill, 1945.

Stamm, Richard. *The Castle: An Illustrated History of the Smithsonian Building,* 2d ed. Washington, DC: Smithsonian Books, 2012.

Stone, Roger D. *The Nature of Development.* New York: Alfred A. Knopf, 1990.

Thompson, Edward K. *A Love Affair with LIFE & Smithsonian.* Columbia: University of Missouri Press, 1995.

Train, Russell E. *Politics, Pollution, and Pandas: An Environmental Memoir.* Washington, DC: Island Press, 2003.

Walker, William S. *A Living Exhibition.* Amherst: University of Massachusetts Press, 2013.

Wilson, E. O., ed. *Biodiversity.* Washington, DC: National Academy Press, 1988.

Winks, Robin. *Cloak and Gown: Scholars in the Secret War, 1939–61.* New Haven, CT: Yale University Press, 1996.

Index

Page numbers in *italics* indicate photos